BEYOND EARTH'S EDGE

BEYOND EARTH'S EDGE

The Poetry of Spaceflight

EDITED BY JULIE SWARSTAD JOHNSON AND
CHRISTOPHER COKINOS

WITH AN INTRODUCTION BY JOHN M. LOGSDON

THE UNIVERSITY OF
ARIZONA PRESS
TUCSON

The University of Arizona Press
www.uapress.arizona.edu

ISBN-13: 978-0-8165-3919-2 (paper)

Cover design by Leigh McDonald
Cover photo: *Shuttle Silhouette*, courtesy of NASA
Designed and typeset by Leigh McDonald in Apollo 10/14 and LeHavre (display)

Captions for the photos in the gallery were adapted from the image sources.

Publication of this book is made possible in part by a grant from the Alfred P. Sloan Foundation
Program in Public Understanding, and by a grant from the Provost's Author Support Fund at the
University of Arizona.

 **ALFRED P. SLOAN FOUNDATION**

Library of Congress Cataloging-in-Publication Data
Names: Johnson, Julie Swarstad, editor. | Cokinos, Christopher, editor. | Logsdon, John M., 1937– writer
    of introduction.
Title: Beyond Earth's edge : the poetry of spaceflight / edited by Julie Swarstad Johnson and Christo-
    pher Cokinos ; with an introduction by John M. Logsdon.
Description: Tucson : University of Arizona Press, 2020.
Identifiers: LCCN 2020010963 | ISBN 9780816539192 (paperback)
Subjects: LCSH: Space flight—Poetry. | American poetry—21st century. | Outer space—Exploration—
    Poetry. | LCGFT: Poetry.
Classification: LCC PS595.O87 B49 2020 | DDC 811/.5408036—dc23
LC record available at https://lccn.loc.gov/2020010963

Printed in the United States of America
♾ This paper meets the requirements of ANSI/NISO Z39.48-1992 (Permanence of Paper).

CONTENTS

APOLLO

ROBOTIC EXPLORERS

PREFACE

When I heard the learn'd astronomer,
When the proofs, the figures, were ranged in columns before me,
When I was shown the charts and diagrams, to add, divide, and measure them,
When I sitting heard the astronomer where he lectured with much applause in
*   the lecture-room,*
How soon unaccountable I became tired and sick,
Till rising and gliding out I wander'd off by myself,
In the mystical moist night-air, and from time to time,
Look'd up in perfect silence at the stars.

— **WALT WHITMAN**

SCIENCE CAN lead us to wonder. Walt Whitman, writing in the nineteenth century, cautions against the sterility of too much time spent with the numbers alone, preferring instead contact with the night. Further reflection reveals that the diagrams, charts, proofs, and figures contain their own beauty as they allow us to uncover the gravitational pull of unseen bodies, the boundaries of our Sun's influence, the shape of a black hole. Through science, we comprehend the universe and can begin to venture out into it; through translations of science into journalism, essays, and especially poetry, we venture out into imagination as well, plumbing the depths of meaning. We encounter the unearthly on those journeys, and like Whitman's speaker, we find ourselves led back to the primacy of wonder. We return to the night sky and everything it contains, seeing anew through scientific exploration the grandeur of the cosmos.

Wonder, and particularly a childlike wonder, is one of the best characteristics of space exploration and spaceflight. Critics of exploration, including especially space exploration, have accused its practitioners of embodying what is called the *puer aeternus* archetype—the eternal child, a boy, who refuses to grow up, who is figuratively and sometimes literally flighty. Embodied best in the figure of Peter Pan, the puer aeternus is restless, searching, and adolescent. The implication is clear: exploration is an ongoing childhood and a refusal of adult responsibilities.

We beg to differ, though some of the poets in this sweeping anthology would not. In an age when adult behavior has put the stability of civilization and the contemporary biosphere at risk, the questioning wonder of children can renew our capacity to better see the present and to imagine a better future. Industrial civilization itself seems trapped in the logic of its own undoing, so looking to space—an enterprise facilitated by industry and technological advancement—seems both natural and troubling. This anthology embraces that paradox as poets, over the past sixty years, have reflected on the promise and peril of spaceflight.

By spaceflight, we mean everything from robotic exploration to human spaceflight in low Earth orbit and beyond, from the launch of Sputnik in 1957 onward. Poets have written earthly (and earthy) responses to these endeavors. They have tried to capture the experiences of astronauts in capsules, on space walks, on the Moon, and back on this home planet. And they have imagined the future. Their poetic response is multivalent, with tones ranging from praise to doubt. The poets themselves hail from diverse backgrounds and orientations. Two writers included here are astronauts. The poems focus primarily on American spaceflight and international events that captivated American imaginations, and as a result, mainly American writers are represented, although some writers hail from the United Kingdom and Canada. Several poems gesture toward non-U.S.-centric viewpoints; a truly international approach merits another anthology, especially as spaceflight becomes an increasingly global undertaking. The voices collected here are transmissions across time and space, and they form an archive of possibility: these poems remind us of how we shepherd ourselves and other life here and maybe elsewhere; they show us what we have done—for ill and for good—and, in doing so, might be part of a celestial navigation system for what seem to be inevitable steps back to the Moon and on to Mars, if not elsewhere. That navigation also can lead us home to Spaceship Earth. We hope future explorers and home-keepers read these poems for their cautions and celebrations.

This anthology arose from an exhibit curated by Julie Swarstad Johnson at the University of Arizona Poetry Center in fall 2016. The breadth, depth, and sheer number of poems on spaceflight she uncovered while creating that exhibit suggests that poets have a significant contribution to make in popular understandings of science and technology. This anthology—the first to focus on the historical sweep of spaceflight through poetry since *Inside Outer Space: New Poems of the Space Age* presented early poetic responses to space exploration in 1970—seeks to illuminate human-directed efforts in space through poets' eyes. Our process in compiling this material was manifold: we read work in prior anthologies, sought collections by poets we knew responded to space, read magazines, dug deep into the library catalog, and asked for advice. The poems are representative of their times, including the pitfalls of their respective cultural moments. As with any such collection, this one has its gaps, including those that resulted from difficulties in obtaining permissions to reprint work. The poems collected here cover numerous aspects of spaceflight from many perspectives, but we look forward to the poems of the future that will explore new directions.

We are grateful to the many people and institutions who helped this book come to fruition, including first and foremost the poets and publishers themselves. To the Alfred P. Sloan Foundation, we extend special thanks for their substantial and crucial support in securing permissions, and for helping us commission renowned historian John M. Logsdon to write his introduction. We could not have completed this project without the Sloan Foundation. We are grateful to the University of Arizona Poetry Center and the Lunar and Planetary Laboratory Space Imagery Center and their staffs for workspace and assistance. The University of Arizona Press has been the ideal partner in publishing. Specifically, we thank Doron Weber, John M. Logsdon, Maria Schuchardt, and especially Kristen Buckles. Julie Swarstad Johnson would like to thank Luke Johnson for his love, support, and proofreading, and she dedicates this book to her parents, who cultivated her love of space, sparked by a memorable visit to Lowell Observatory. Christopher Cokinos would like to thank Kathe Lison for her support and love, and he dedicates this work to his sister, Vicki, with love and with memories of watching *Star Trek*.

Julie Swarstad Johnson and Christopher Cokinos
Tucson, Arizona
May 2019

EXPLORING THE UNKNOWN

The United States in Space

JOHN M. LOGSDON

THE POEMS in this volume reflect many perspectives on one of the most significant developments of the twentieth century—the extension of human activity off the surface of Earth into outer space. Historian Arthur Schlesinger Jr. in 1999 suggested "the one thing for which this century will be remembered 500 years from now is: This was the century when we began the exploration of space." Going into space has many objectives—excitement, discovery, power, pride, commerce, and utility among them. This brief essay reviews the evolution of U.S. space activities over the past six decades to provide a background useful for understanding and appreciating the works and images included in this volume.

Since the first two artificial Earth satellites were launched in fall 1957, more than eight thousand objects have been sent into orbit and beyond, more by the United States than any other country. In addition to robotic satellites and probes, as of April 2019 some 565 humans have made the trip, some multiple times; just 24 have gone beyond Earth orbit, traveling to the Moon and back. There are currently plans for humans to return to the Moon, then travel to Mars. A variety of public and private actors today see space as a frontier, the exploration and exploitation of which is only beginning.

The purposes of government and private-sector activity in space range from the practical to the visionary. Satellites have proven excellent and profitable devices for relaying voice, video, and data communications around the globe; for observing patterns on the land, the oceans, and the atmosphere that can be used to forecast a wide variety of phenomena; for providing the positioning, navigation, and timing information needed to operate a modern economy; for enhancing military power; and for observing activities around the world related to a nation's security. Earth-orbiting satellites and robotic probes leaving Earth orbit have made scientific discoveries that have rewritten textbooks and given us exciting looks at our solar system neighbors. Some space missions have addressed questions that go to the core of human curiosity: Where have we come from? What is the fate of Earth, the solar system, and the cosmos? Are we alone?

As Schlesinger suggested two decades ago, space exploration is one of the great human adventures of modern civilization. It is thus not surprising that it has motivated the kind of creative work represented in this volume. These poems are a representative sampling of the verbal imagery resulting from the idea of, and the reality of, space exploration. In addition, the volume contains a sampling of the many thousands of striking visual images resulting from humans sending themselves and their machines into orbit and beyond. Seeing for ourselves close-up views of other worlds in our solar system, of other stars in addition to our Sun—some in the process of creation and others as they die and collapse into black holes—and of millions of galaxies beyond the Milky Way has reshaped humanity's perspective on its place in the cosmos in ways both humbling and profound. With the images sent back from deep in space, people on Earth participate in what historian Daniel Boorstin has called "public discovery"—sharing with human and robotic explorers what they are seeing at nearly the moment they first see it. They have also seen Earth in numerous pictures taken in orbit and beyond, reminding us of its unique character (at least in this solar system) and the need to cherish and preserve it.

THE ORIGINS OF U.S. SPACE ACTIVITY

Human activity in space and on other planets has been a frequent focus of fictional writing since at least the mid-nineteenth century, and science fiction writers such as Jules Verne, H. G. Wells, and later Robert Heinlein, Arthur C. Clarke, Ray Bradbury, and many others, were widely read. Comic strips and television series such as *Buck Rogers* and *Flash Gordon* were also popular. German émigré rocket pioneer Wernher von Braun, who had been brought to the United States after World War II, became during the 1950s an effective popularizer of the idea of space travel. He worked with Walt Disney to produce television accounts suggesting the imminence of humans going into space and with the news magazine *Collier's* to describe trips to the Moon and Mars in such technical detail that they seemed eminently feasible. Many of the magazine's articles were vividly illustrated by artists such as Chesley Bonestell. The idea that space travel was just around the corner was embodied in Disneyland's Tomorrowland, which opened in 1955, reflecting its acceptance as part of American popular culture. Thus the first forays into orbit did not come as a surprise to most in the United States.

What did surprise most Americans was that it was their Cold War rival, the Soviet Union, that was first to space. The USSR launched the first satellite, Sputnik-1 ("fellow traveler" in Russian), on October 4, 1957. A month later, Sputnik-2 carried Laika, a mongrel dog found on the streets of Moscow, on a one-way trip to orbit. These two first satellites were intended to demonstrate to the world that the Soviet Union had become the first spacefaring nation, and incidentally also had the rocket power to send a nuclear warhead over intercontinental distances. These missions constituted a significant propaganda success for the Soviet Union in its Cold War competition with the United States for global geopolitical leadership.

The United States responded to the challenge of the Sputniks by creating a new civilian space agency, the National Aeronautics and Space Administration (NASA), and charging it with "the expansion of human knowledge of phenomena in the atmosphere and space," "the establishment of long-range studies of the potential benefits to be gained from, the opportunities for, and the problems involved in the utilization of . . . space activities for peaceful and scientific purposes," and "the preservation of the role of the United States as a leader in . . . space science and technology." Since beginning operation in October 1958, NASA has responded to this mandate by carrying out a comprehensive program of space science, space applications, and space exploration. In 1961, President John F. Kennedy added to NASA's responsibilities, making the agency a key tool of national security policy by establishing the goal of U.S. preeminence in space as an element of U.S. power and prestige. Mobilizing the space agency to serve this core national interest has had a lasting effect on the expectations placed on NASA and the political context within which it operates. NASA is not "just another" government agency; it carries the burden of representing American excellence both domestically and internationally.

Although a thriving commercial space sector organized around the launching and operation of communications satellites has emerged in the past thirty years and a commercial Earth observation business is emerging, most other U.S. space activities to date are still carried out under government sponsorship. Space systems have proven effective tools for national security purposes, and the current government budget for military- and intelligence-related space activities is actually larger than NASA's budget for civilian space activities. In recent years, the advent of several high-profile and wealthy individuals interested in both space commerce and space exploration has spurred a "new space" movement that could change the balance between public- and private-sector space efforts. Until (and if) that happens, NASA will have the lead role in U.S. civilian space activities.

Of those activities, three resonate with the contents of this volume: (1) human spaceflight, (2) robotic exploration of the solar system, and (3) space-based observations of the universe. The following sections of this essay discuss each of these areas.

HUMANS IN SPACE

During the first years after Sputnik, President Dwight D. Eisenhower downplayed the significance of U.S. space leadership, although he did grudgingly approve Project Mercury, the initial U.S. human spaceflight effort. This priority changed soon after John F. Kennedy became president on January 20, 1961. Kennedy had not paid much attention to the space program prior to coming to the White House and was initially uncertain about what priority to give NASA. That uncertainty quickly disappeared. On April 12, 1961, the Soviet Union sent cosmonaut Yuri Gagarin on a one-orbit flight in his Vostok (East) spacecraft, and the world reaction was uniformly positive. Once again, the United States was second in a highly visible space achievement. To the highly competitive young president, this was not acceptable. Within a few days, he asked his advisers to identify "a space program which promises dramatic results in which we could win."

"WE SHOULD GO TO THE MOON"

The answer was quick to appear—send Americans to the Moon. The existing Soviet rocket was not powerful enough to send cosmonauts to the lunar surface. Wernher von Braun, who had gone to work for NASA in 1960, told the White House that the United States could compete with the USSR to build such a booster and the other equipment required for a lunar landing mission, with at least a fifty-fifty chance of being first. Kennedy's advisers told him that the prestige that would result from beating the Soviet Union to the Moon was "part of the battle along the fluid front of the Cold War." Kennedy accepted this recommendation, announcing before a joint session of Congress on May 25, 1961, a national goal of a lunar landing "before this decade is out." Project Apollo—the race to the Moon—was on.

Setting the challenging lunar landing objective had a profound effect on all of NASA's programs. The goal became preeminence—a clearly leading position—in all areas of space activity. In the months after Kennedy's speech, the NASA budget was increased by 89 percent. It went up 101 percent the following year, and 40 percent the next. At the peak of Apollo, NASA received more than 4 percent of the government budget and had 35,000 employees assisted by 400,000 contractor employees. NASA created the Manned Spacecraft Center in Houston to manage Project Apollo and constructed a massive launch complex on Merritt Island, Florida, adjacent to Cape Canaveral, for Apollo's powerful Moon rocket. This was a war-like but peaceful mobilization of financial and human resources aimed at achieving clear space leadership in both human and robotic spaceflight.

Despite his public rhetoric, Kennedy's decision to go to the Moon was motivated not by the romance of space exploration but by a calculated judgment that leading in space achievement was an important aspect of the Cold War competition between the United States and the Soviet Union. In a secretly recorded conversation in November 1962, he said "the Soviet Union has made this [space achievement] a test of the system. . . . This is, whether we like it or not, in a sense a race. . . . Everything we do ought really to be tied into getting onto the Moon ahead of the Russians."

Between 1961 and 1966, there were six flights in Project Mercury (two suborbital and four orbital) and ten flights in the two-person Project Gemini, established in 1962 to gain the experience in rendezvous, extra-vehicle activity, and long-duration flight critical to Apollo. Mercury astronaut John Glenn, as he prepared for the first U.S. orbital flight in late 1961, found that NASA was not planning to include a camera in the equipment he would be carrying aboard his Friendship 7 spacecraft. Glenn used his own money to purchase a simple camera in a Florida drugstore and had it modified so he could operate it while in orbit, thereby establishing the practice of astronaut photography that has persisted since.

As NASA prepared to begin Apollo flights, a tragic fire during a launch pad test on January 27, 1967, killed astronauts Virgil "Gus" Grissom, Edward White, and Roger Chaffee. This accident served as a wakeup call to NASA and its contractors that changes in the

Apollo program were needed; in the subsequent months, much of the Apollo spacecraft was redesigned, leading to its first orbital test during the October 1968 Apollo 7 mission. Then a bold and risky decision led to the Apollo 8 mission going into orbit around the Moon on Christmas Eve 1968; as they became the first humans to circle the Moon, the crew read from the first verses of the book of Genesis.

With the path to the Moon open, Apollo 9 and Apollo 10 were successful test flights, leading to the historic landing of Apollo 11 Lunar Module Eagle at Tranquility Base in July 1969. Neil Armstrong took "one small step for [a] man, one giant leap for mankind." The image of Buzz Aldrin standing next to the American flag on the lunar surface has become a lasting symbol of the best of American achievement, even as the plaque left behind on the Lunar Module read, "We came in peace for all mankind."

Six more Apollo missions followed; five were successful, but a spacecraft explosion prevented the April 1970 Apollo 13 mission from reaching the Moon, nearly leading to the deaths of the astronaut crew. Two planned lunar landings were cancelled, as both a money-saving and a risk-reducing measure. Leftover Apollo equipment was used during the 1970s for Skylab, an experimental space station, and the Apollo-Soyuz Test Project, the first meeting in orbit of American astronauts and Soviet cosmonauts and the ceremonial end to the Space Race.

THE END OF HUMAN EXPLORATION

As Apollo 17 left the Moon on December 14, 1972, President Richard Nixon issued a statement suggesting that "this may be the last time in this century that men will walk on the Moon." By his post-Apollo decisions President Nixon made this forecast reality. He was acutely tuned to public opinion, and he told the head of NASA in January 1970 that "the polls and the people to whom he talked indicated to him that the mood of the people was for cuts in space." This was an accurate reading of public sentiment. Even during the run up to the lunar landing in the 1960s, public support for human spaceflight had been intermittent. Enthusiasm swelled during the actual spaceflights of the Mercury, Gemini, and early Apollo missions, but that interest quickly dissipated between flights. The Apollo 11 landing was celebrated worldwide, but the excitement was short-lived. By the Apollo 13 mission in April 1970 (until the crew's lives were in danger), the major television networks had ended their live coverage. Even flying to the Moon could not sustain public interest.

Apollo had been defined as a race to get to the Moon first. Once that race had been won, there was no compelling reason to continue a space program of the pace and expense of Apollo. The power of Kennedy's commitment to reach the Moon "before this decade is out," combined with the undertaking becoming a memorial to a fallen young president, had been enough to carry Apollo through to meeting Kennedy's goal, but was insufficient to sustain a continuing program of human flights beyond Earth orbit.

Reflecting this reality, in March 1970 Richard Nixon declared that "space expenditures must take their proper place within a rigorous system of national priorities. . . . What we do in space from here on in must become a normal and regular part of our national life." This has been the governing U.S. space policy since, and the result is a space program lacking the political and financial support to undertake new voyages of human exploration. The NASA budget had been almost 5 percent of government expenditures in the mid-1960s; Nixon put NASA on a path to reduce its budget share to 1 percent or less. NASA currently commands less than 0.5 percent of federal spending.

HUMAN SPACEFLIGHT SINCE APOLLO

In its planning for programs to follow Project Apollo, NASA suggested a goal of human missions to Mars in the 1980s. That ambition was quickly squelched by the Nixon White House. As first steps toward Mars, NASA proposed developing during the 1970s a permanently occupied twelve-person space station in low Earth orbit, serviced by a reusable vehicle that would travel back and forth to the station with crew and supplies—a space shuttle. But the Nixon administration was also not willing to approve simultaneous development of these two programs. NASA decided that if a space shuttle were developed first it could serve other purposes until such a time as a space station was available. On January 5, 1972, President Nixon announced he had approved the space shuttle, saying it "will revolutionize transportation into near space by routinizing it. It will take the astronomical costs out of astronautics." These words put an unachievable burden on the shuttle program from its start.

The space shuttle was to be a combination of partially reusable launch vehicle and short-duration space station. It could carry up to seven astronauts and large and heavy payloads into low Earth orbit, then stay there for up to two weeks, deploying satellites to various orbits and carrying out experiments and observations in the space environment. The shuttle orbiter was a winged vehicle that could glide to a runway landing and be refurbished for reuse. The shuttle was to be launched forty or more times a year, carrying all U.S. government payloads and the satellites of other countries and commercial space companies.

The first flight of the space shuttle took place on April 12, 1981, several years behind schedule. Then, on January 25, 1984, President Ronald Reagan announced his approval of a space station, though one more modest than NASA had proposed fifteen years earlier. With that approval, the elements of the space infrastructure that would operate in low Earth orbit for the foreseeable future could be put in place. Reagan invited U.S. "friends and allies" to participate in the space-station program, and Canada, Japan, and several European countries accepted that invitation.

In the mid-1980s the shuttle program was operating according to the premises set out when it was approved in 1972—that it was capable of frequent, routine, and affordable operation and safe enough to fly non-astronauts. Those premises were rudely shattered on January 28, 1986, when shuttle Challenger was engulfed in a fireball seventy-three seconds after launch and broke apart. The seven-person crew, including "teacher-in-space" Christa McAuliffe, died. In the aftermath of the accident, NASA was ordered by the White House to stop using the shuttle to launch commercial payloads.

Meanwhile the space-station program, which had been named Freedom, moved forward slowly. By the early 1990s it was teetering on the verge of cancellation. After the collapse of the Soviet Union, new President Bill Clinton in 1993 decided to invite Russia into the space-station partnership. The existing station partners agreed with this initiative, and the station designation was changed to International Space Station (ISS). Bringing Russia into the station program provided enough political support to ensure the program would continue. By November 2000 the ISS was ready for initial habitation; it has been permanently occupied by astronauts, cosmonauts, and even a few visiting space tourists ever since. Humans have now been living in space continuously for more than two decades.

By the late 1990s, the space shuttle had become what was originally intended: a system for assembling and servicing the space station. Only occasionally did the shuttle carry out missions not related to the ISS. On one of those missions, scheduled to land on February 1, 2003, shuttle orbiter Columbia broke apart as it reentered Earth's atmosphere. Once again, seven crewmembers died. There were calls from many in Congress and the media to immediately retire the shuttle, but the ISS was not yet completely assembled, with elements from Europe and Japan yet to be launched. In late 2003, President George W. Bush decided to keep the shuttle flying until ISS assembly was complete, then scheduled for 2010. Assembly and outfitting of the ISS was not completed until July 2011; at that point, the space shuttle fleet was retired from service.

During its thirty years of operation, the space shuttle was launched 135 times. It carried 355 different people, 306 men and 49 women, into orbit, and deployed a wide range of scientific, commercial, and national security payloads. It made five flights to service the Hubble Space Telescope and thirty-seven flights dedicated to ISS assembly and outfitting. As the first partially reusable crew-carrying spacecraft, the shuttle was a technological marvel. But it was very expensive to operate, averaging more than $1 billion per launch. Instead of launching forty or more times a year as originally intended, it never carried out more than nine flights in a single year.

Since 2011, the ISS has continued operation, carrying out a variety of research efforts. It has been staffed by a mixture of astronauts and cosmonauts from the ISS partners who stay aboard for months at a time. One byproduct of the ongoing presence of humans in orbit is a continuing stream of engaging images of Earth and its atmosphere taken by the onboard crew; another is frequent opportunities for interactions between the crew in orbit and various audiences on Earth. No date for the end of ISS operations has been agreed upon; one possibility suggested by NASA is for a private-sector organization to assume control of the ISS. It is also possible that the ISS will be deorbited as no longer worth the multi-billion-dollar annual cost of keeping it in operation.

RETURN TO THE MOON?

America's human spaceflight activities have for forty-eight years been limited to low Earth orbit. Beginning in the mid-1980s, several proposals have been made to resume journeys into deep space, and particularly to return to the Moon. A presidentially appointed National Commission on Space in 1986 set forth a fifty-year plan for settling the Moon and Mars, but in the aftermath of the Challenger accident political interest all but disappeared. On the twentieth anniversary of the first lunar landing, July 20, 1989, President George H. W. Bush called for a return to the Moon, "this time to stay." His administration tried for several years to gather support for what became called the Space Exploration Initiative, but with no success; the plan was stillborn. On January 14, 2004, President George W. Bush set forth a Vision for Space Exploration that called for a return to the Moon. The program to implement that vision was called Constellation; in 2010 President Barack Obama cancelled that program and instead proposed skipping the Moon and making Mars the destination for human spaceflight. Although NASA worked on a new large launch vehicle and a new spacecraft for deep-space journeys during the Obama presidency, progress was slow. Then in December 2017 President Donald Trump signed a policy directive saying that "the United States will lead the return of humans to the Moon for long-term exploration and utilization, followed by human missions to Mars and other destinations." In March 2019, Vice President Mike Pence, who has special responsibility for space matters, declared "it is the stated policy of this administration and the United States of America to return American astronauts to the Moon within the next five years."

Whether the current push to return to the Moon will suffer the fate of predecessor initiatives, or whether Americans will return to the Moon in this decade, is not clear at the time of this writing. But it does seem certain that if government-sponsored human spaceflight is to survive, it must give priority to resuming travel beyond low Earth orbit to the Moon, Mars, and perhaps beyond.

WHAT ABOUT THE SPACE BILLIONAIRES?

NASA's U.S. monopoly on human spaceflight has in recent years been challenged by the emergence of wealthy, high-profile individuals who have set out visions of moving humans off Earth to distant destinations. The most well-known of these are Jeff Bezos and Elon Musk.

Bezos, founder of the online merchandiser Amazon, is the world's wealthiest individual. In 2000, Bezos founded a space company, Blue Origin, which operates with the motto *Gradatim Ferociter* (Step by Step, Ferociously). Blue Origin is indeed slowly but steadily developing comprehensive human-spaceflight capabilities, with the stated purpose of "building a road to space with our reusable launch vehicles, so our children can build the future." That future, says Bezos, will involve humanity expanding beyond Earth to harness the energy and other resources of the solar system. If this vision becomes reality, Bezos anticipates, much Earth-bound industry will be moved off the planet and millions of people will be living and working in space.

Musk gleaned his initial wealth through helping develop and then selling his share in the internet-based application PayPal, and in 2002 founded Space Exploration Technologies (SpaceX), with an initial goal of lowering the cost of access to space by developing reusable launch vehicles. His company has met that objective and has become a disruptive force in the space launch arena. SpaceX has also in recent years developed cargo and crew-carrying spacecraft. In 2016 Musk laid out a vision of developing the interplanetary transport capabilities to help create a million-person city on Mars. In leading SpaceX and other technology-based entrepreneurial ventures, Musk has created an iconic identity that has attracted the attention and enthusiasm of many young individuals.

Bezos, Musk, and a growing number of other entrepreneurs have excited many people who want to be involved in space activities but are weary of the slow pace of those activities as they are being carried out under government sponsorship. Whether this "new space" excitement can be sustained as their ventures move from the practical to the visionary, and whether their private sector–led activities can partner productively with continuing government space efforts, will be challenges to be faced in coming years.

ROBOTIC SCIENCE AND EXPLORATION

Issues related to human spaceflight have been addressed at the highest level of the U.S. government. In contrast, the U.S. scientific community has since NASA's beginnings had strong influence over the objectives and content of U.S. space science and exploration efforts, setting the agenda for political authorities to implement. In particular, over the past forty years reports prepared under the auspices of the nongovernmental National Academy of Sciences have laid out scientific priorities in various sectors of space science such as planetary exploration and astrophysics, and NASA has generally followed those priorities in proposing missions to the White House and Congress. The challenge facing NASA in selecting which missions to undertake has been to balance the scientific community's ambitions with the funding available for space science. The result has been a mixture of small, mid-sized, and ambitious and expensive "flagship" missions.

EXPLORING THE SOLAR SYSTEM

In the May 8, 1961, memorandum recommending that President Kennedy set a lunar landing as a national goal, NASA Administrator James Webb and Secretary of Defense Robert McNamara wrote, "It is man, not merely machines, that captures the imagination of the world." This observation may have been valid for Apollo but has not been borne out in the years since. Repetitive stays in low Earth orbit by astronauts aboard the space shuttle and now the International Space Station have attracted little continuing public attention. More interesting to the general public from the 1970s on, and likely more productive scientifically, have been the many U.S. robotic missions traveling away from Earth into the solar system, sending back to Earth spectacular images of celestial bodies along with textbook-changing data. The U.S. solar system program is true exploration, defined as "going to a place to learn about it."

As of the start of 2020 the United States had launched more than one hundred spacecraft beyond Earth orbit. Those probes have visited the near vicinity of the Sun, orbited and landed on Earth's Moon, and flown by every planet and many of their moons. American spacecraft have orbited Mercury, Venus, Mars, Jupiter, and Saturn. Eight U.S. spacecraft have landed on Mars, six of them carrying rovers that explored areas near their landing sites. The New Horizons probe flew by Pluto in 2015, sending back vivid images of a body that had previously been only dimly observed. Then, on January 1, 2019, the same spacecraft flew by an oddly shaped object called Arrokoth in the Kuiper Belt at the outer reaches of the solar system, 4.1 billion miles distant from Earth. Other U.S. probes have landed on asteroids, sent an impactor into a comet to study its composition, and brought back to Earth samples of cometary dust.

These probes carry cameras of increasing capabilities that have given us memorable images, among others, of the cratered surface of Mercury, of the traces of the six Apollo expeditions on the surface of the Moon, the snow caps at the poles of Mars contrasted with the Red Planet's varied canyons and mountains, the violent storm that we see as a red spot on Jupiter, erupting volcanoes on Jupiter's moon Io and Saturn's moon Enceladus, the icy surface of Jupiter's moon Europa covering a water ocean that might harbor life, the filigree character of Saturn's rings, methane lakes on Saturn's large moon Titan, the featureless surface of Uranus, Neptune's icy blue and windy cloud cover, and a heart-shaped plain on the surface of Pluto. Those images, more than seeing astronauts living aboard the ISS, have highlighted U.S. space accomplishments since the end of Apollo.

MARS AS A FOCUS

As the most Earth-like body in the solar system, and one that has possibly supported life forms (and even possibly still does have extant life), Mars has been a primary focus of the U.S. planetary exploration program. The Mariner 4 spacecraft flew by Mars in July 1965, returning images that showed a cratered, seemingly dead world that disappointed those hoping to find signs of life. Mariner 9 in 1971 was the first spacecraft to orbit Mars; images it sent back transformed the perception of Mars from a barren planet to a world full of past geological activity and a place that once had plentiful amounts of water. Two landers, Viking 1 and Viking 2, arrived on Mars in 1976; each was accompanied by an orbiting spacecraft. The Viking missions gave a detailed view of Mars, but the experiments intended to find evidence of life did not produce definitive results.

There were no U.S. missions to Mars between Viking and a 1992 spacecraft that failed as it entered Mars orbit. Since then, the United States has succeeded in sending four orbiters (Mars Global Surveyor, Mars Odyssey, Mars Reconnaissance Orbiter, and Mars Atmosphere and Volatile Evolution, a.k.a. MAVEN), three landers (Mars Pathfinder, Phoenix, and InSight), and four rovers (Sojourner, Spirit, Opportunity, and Curiosity) to explore the Red Planet. Additional missions will follow, with the return to Earth of samples of Martian soil planned late in the 2020s. Much about Mars is now understood, including the presence of significant amounts of water, but the most fundamental questions—Was there ever life on Mars? Does life persist there today?—have not yet been answered. There is more to explore on Mars.

THE OUTER PLANETS

NASA's first missions to the outer planets were the small spacecraft Pioneer 10 and Pioneer 11, launched in the early 1970s to fly by Jupiter and, in the case of Pioneer 11, also Saturn. As NASA in the late 1960s considered its next outer-planet missions, Gary Flandro of the Jet Propulsion Laboratory discovered that in the 1970s and

1980s the five outer planets, from Jupiter to Pluto, would be in an alignment that would allow a spacecraft to fly by each body on a single mission. This alignment occurs only once every 175 years. That trajectory was dubbed the Grand Tour. A dedicated Grand Tour mission was too ambitious for the post-Apollo NASA, but a more modest version was approved and named Voyager. Because of their different planned trajectories, Voyager 2 was launched on August 20, 1977, and Voyager 1, on September 5, 1977. Voyager 1 flew by Jupiter and its moons in 1979 and the Saturnian system in 1980 on a trajectory that carried it into interstellar space in 2012. On its way out of the solar system, it pivoted to allow its camera to record an image of the distant Earth, characterized as a "pale blue dot" in the vastness of space. Voyager 2 also visited Jupiter and Saturn, but then completed most of the Grand Tour, flying by Uranus in 1986 and Neptune in 1989. It is still the only space-craft to visit those two planets. The Voyager 2 spacecraft entered interstellar space in 2018. Among their many scientific discoveries, the two spacecraft discovered active volcanoes on one of Jupiter's moons and explored the intricate patterns of Saturn's rings. Both Voyager spacecraft carried greetings to any form of life, should it ever be encountered, on a twelve-inch gold-plated copper record containing sounds and images selected to portray the diversity of life and culture on Earth. (No poems were included.) The contents of the record were chosen by a committee chaired by astronomer and science popularizer Carl Sagan of Cornell University. Sagan and his associates assembled 115 images and a variety of natural sounds. To this they added musical selections from different cultures and eras, as well as spoken greetings in fifty-five languages.

The next step in the sequence of planetary exploration after a flyby was a mission to orbit a planet. The Galileo spacecraft was launched in 1989 and orbited Jupiter and its moons between 1995 and 2003; among its many discoveries, Galileo identified the water ocean of Jupiter's moon Europa as a potential venue for organic life. A second orbiter, Juno, began its mission at Jupiter in 2016. The Cassini spacecraft, launched in 1997, completed 294 orbits through the Saturnian system between 2004 and 2017. It carried a European-built probe called Huygens, which descended to

Saturn's large moon Titan in 2005. The Cassini mission revealed the complexity of Saturn, its rings, and its many moons, discovering active volcanoes and possible indications of organic life on Saturn's moon Enceladus.

As noted above, NASA's New Horizons spacecraft flew by Pluto in 2015, completing the initial reconnaissance of the solar system. In addition, U.S. spacecraft have visited several asteroids in the belt between Mars and Jupiter and encountered comets on their journeys through the inner solar system. The solar system images produced by NASA spacecraft over the past decades remain a source of wonder at the beauty and diversity of Earth's nearest neighbors.

OBSERVATORIES IN ORBIT AND BEYOND

Increasingly sophisticated ground-based telescopes have been since the 1800s essential tools for astronomers as they investigated the Milky Way galaxy and the myriad galaxies in the universe beyond. Once it became possible to place telescopes into outer space, researchers were eager to begin observations above Earth's atmosphere, since it distorts or blocks radiation in various parts of the electromagnetic spectrum coming from distant objects in the cosmos. NASA began to launch astronomical observatories in the 1970s, the best known of which were labeled "the Great Observatories":

· Hubble Space Telescope, named for Edwin Hubble, who discovered the expansion of the universe. Hubble observes in the visible, ultraviolet, and infrared regions of the spectrum. It was launched on April 24, 1990, and, after five missions to repair and update it, is still in operation.
· Compton Gamma Ray Observatory, named for Arthur H. Compton, a pioneer in gamma-ray studies. It was launched on April 5, 1991, and was deorbited on June 4, 2000.
· Chandra X-ray Observatory, named for Subrahmanyan Chandrasekhar, who defined the upper mass limit for a white dwarf star. It was launched on July 23, 1999, and is still operating.

- Spitzer Space Telescope, named for Lyman Spitzer, who proposed the concept of orbiting observatories as long ago as 1946 and campaigned for such missions from the 1950s through the 1970s. It observed the cosmos in the infrared frequencies. Spitzer was launched on August 25, 2003; its operations were terminated on January 30, 2020.

Each of these telescopes has made major discoveries related to the origin, evolution, and current state of the universe. Hubble is the best known of the four because it operates in the visible region of the spectrum and thus produces dramatic and easily understood images (for example, the "Pillars of Creation" image of star formation in the Eagle Nebula and various "deep field" images showing the many galaxies in the universe). Originally launched in 1990 with a misshapen mirror, astronauts during a dramatic 1993 repair mission installed corrective optics, restoring its intended capabilities. Four other servicing missions have extended Hubble's service life and improved its observing power.

NASA has launched several other astrophysical missions that have made significant discoveries. For example, George Smoot and John Mather won the 2006 Nobel Prize for their work on NASA's Cosmic Background Explorer, which provided evidence in support of the Big Bang theory of the origin of the universe. Between 2009 and 2018, the Kepler Space Telescope, named after Renaissance astronomer Johannes Kepler, discovered thousands of exoplanets—planets orbiting around a star in the Milky Way galaxy other than the Sun. Future astrophysics missions, particularly the multibillion dollar James Webb Space Telescope planned for launch in 2021, will search for exoplanets that may harbor life and explore issues such as the nature of dark matter and dark energy and the nature of space, time, and matter at the edges of black holes.

IMAGES

There are many scientific, political, cultural, social, and economic legacies of U.S. space activities over the past sixty years. This brief essay can only hint at the scope of those legacies and their lasting effects. There is also a legacy of images associated with going into space. Indeed, the poems in this volume are a representative sampling of the verbal imagery resulting from the idea and the reality of space exploration.

Of all the *visual* images resulting from space exploration, perhaps the most iconic is the "Earthrise" photo of the bright blue, cloud-streaked planet rising over the stark lunar landscape taken by Apollo 8 crewmember Bill Anders as he orbited the Moon on Christmas Eve 1968. Anders later commented, "We came all the way to the Moon, but discovered the Earth." The poet Archibald MacLeish, writing in the *New York Times* on the occasion of the Apollo 8 mission, suggested that

> to see the earth as it truly is, small and blue and beautiful in that eternal silence where it floats, is to see ourselves as riders on the earth together, brothers on that bright loveliness in the eternal cold—brothers who know now they are truly brothers.

If a shared consciousness of human interdependence on Spaceship Earth were to result from looking back toward home while exploring outer space, that legacy alone might justify the effort.

On February 20, 1962, John Glenn became the first American to orbit Earth in the Mercury capsule named Friendship 7 (for the seven original Mercury astronauts). He carried a drugstore camera to take photos of the views, such as this one, which he declared were "beautiful." He orbited three times in about five hours. (NASA)

The first human mission to reach the Moon, but not its surface, Apollo 8 is famous for the crew's Christmas Eve 1968 recitation of the opening of the book of Genesis and for this photo—now called "Earthrise"—taken by Bill Anders. The mission commander, Frank Borman, originally objected to having cameras on board. "Earthrise" helped spark the modern environmental movement. (NASA)

One of the iconic images of the 1969 Apollo 11 mission, Buzz Aldrin stands by the American flag and the Lunar Module. Aldrin, the second human to walk on the Moon's surface, called the lunar vistas "magnificent desolation." (NASA)

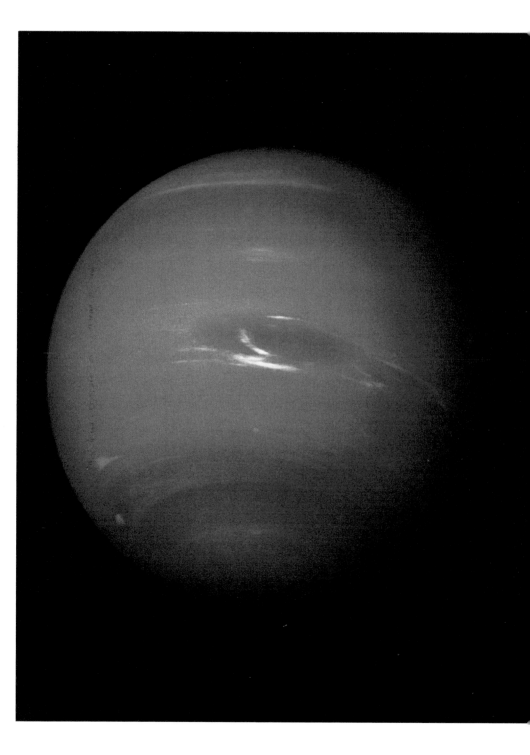

This picture of Neptune was produced from the last whole planet images taken through the green and orange filters on the Voyager 2 narrow-angle camera while the spacecraft was 4.4 million miles from the planet, four days and twenty hours before closest approach in the summer of 1989. This image shows the Great Dark Spot and its companion bright smudge; on the west limb the fast-moving bright feature called Scooter and the smaller "Dark Spot 2" are visible. (NASA/JPL)

Suggested by Carl Sagan, this 1990 image of Earth was taken by Voyager 1 at a distance of 4 billion miles as the craft traversed the outer solar system on its eventual way to interstellar space. The probe was launched in 1977. Sagan said of the photograph, "Our planet is a lonely speck in the great enveloping cosmic dark. In our obscurity, in all this vastness, there is no hint that help will come from elsewhere to save us from ourselves." (NASA/JPL)

Composed of images taken by the Galileo spacecraft in 1995 and 1998, this reprocessed image of the icy Jovian moon Europa shows cracks, ridges, "microchaos," and more. We now believe that Europa, like several other moons in the solar system, is an ocean world. Due to heat caused by Jupiter's gravitational push-and-pull, there is liquid salt water beneath the ice, water that may contain life. (NASA/JPL-Caltech/SETI Institute)

Hubble Space Telescope has arguably been the most important observatory ever built. Orbiting above Earth's atmosphere, Hubble was launched in 1990 with flawed optics, later corrected by space walks from the Space Shuttle in one of NASA's finest hours. The correction allowed for images such as these, a "deep field" that shows a tiny portion of sky that looks back more than 13 billion years to show so many fossil galaxies they appear to be swarming. (NASA, ESA, G. Illingworth, D. Magee, and P. Oesch [University of California, Santa Cruz], R. Bouwens [Leiden University], and the HUDF09 Team)

These towering tendrils of cosmic dust and gas, stretching roughly four to five light-years, sit at the heart of M16, or the Eagle Nebula, captured here by Hubble Space Telescope in 2014 to kick off the telescope's twenty-fifth year in orbit. The aptly named "Pillars of Creation" are part of an active star-forming region and hide newborn stars in their wispy columns, bathed in scorching ultraviolent light from a cluster of young stars located just outside the frame. (NASA, ESA, and the Hubble Heritage Teams [STScI/AURA])

Captured by NASA's New Horizons spacecraft in July 2015, this high-resolution enhanced color view of Pluto combines blue, red, and infrared images. Pluto's surface sports a remarkable range of subtle colors, enhanced in this view to a rainbow of pale blues, yellows, oranges, and deep reds. Many landforms have their own distinct colors, telling a complex geological and climatological story that scientists have only just begun to decode. (NASA/Johns Hopkins University Applied Physics Laboratory/ Southwest Research Institute)

Taken by HiRISE (High Resolution Imaging Science Experiment) aboard the Mars Reconnaissance Orbiter in late 2018, this image reveals the geologic history of Mars, written in its exposed layers. Erosion on the surface of Mars exposes several shades of light toned layers, likely sedimentary deposits, while the most recent geologic features are the narrow sand dunes snaking across the top. (NASA/JPL-Caltech/University of Arizona)

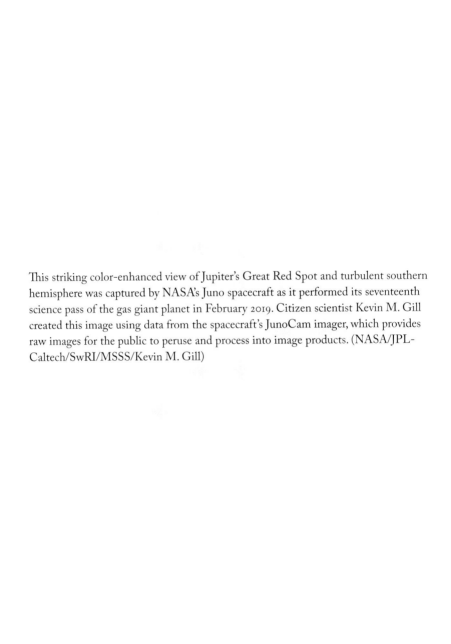

This striking color-enhanced view of Jupiter's Great Red Spot and turbulent southern hemisphere was captured by NASA's Juno spacecraft as it performed its seventeenth science pass of the gas giant planet in February 2019. Citizen scientist Kevin M. Gill created this image using data from the spacecraft's JunoCam imager, which provides raw images for the public to peruse and process into image products. (NASA/JPL-Caltech/SwRI/MSSS/Kevin M. Gill)

SPUTNIK AND THE RACE TO THE MOON

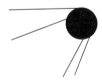

O
RIGINS BLOSSOM and recede like fire and smoke from engine exhaust.

When does the Space Age begin—or begin to begin? With Icarus flying too close to the Sun? With the Montgolfiers and the first human flights—in hot-air balloons—over astonished crowds in France? With the Wright brothers and those who followed with the rapid development of powered flight, higher and higher? Did the Space Age begin in the imagination of an obscure Russian teacher, Konstantin Tsiolkovsky, who foresaw rocket-propelled travel outside the atmosphere, and with the first crude mechanical rockets launched by the American Robert Goddard between 1926 and 1941? Or did the Space Age begin in the imaginations of such writers as Jules Verne and H. G. Wells, each of whom sent humans to the Moon in their Victorian-era novels?

A closer source: the Nazi rocket launches during the last gasps of WWII, when Adolf Hitler ordered V-2 rockets, the first long-range ballistic missiles, to be launched against England and other targets. Those missiles were manufactured and assembled by concentration-camp labor with the direct knowledge of Wernher von Braun, Arthur Rudolph, and other members of the German rocket team that the U.S. government captured to hasten American development of such vehicles. The V-2 slaves worked in an underground factory. The Space Age, there and then, begins in pain and darkness. The failure to fully acknowledge this history should haunt all of us who dream of space.

David Simons, an Air Force doctor, didn't just dream of space. He wanted to be an astronaut as the United States began to plan seriously for human flight above the atmosphere—and he saw space without officially becoming a Mercury astronaut. For Project Manhigh, which took place between 1955 and 1958, Simons flew in a tiny pressurized capsule under a stratospheric balloon—testing human reactions to such confinement and to cosmic rays—and saw, with his own eyes, the curve of Earth. Along with secret X-1 test pilot Kit Murray in 1954, Simons was one of the first humans to do so.

But conventional wisdom says that the Space Age began on October 4, 1957, when the Russians launched an "artificial moon" called Sputnik. This came as—to put it mildly—a shock to the American people, and the Space Race began in earnest. American rockets blew up, leading to jokes about "Kaputnik," but once Explorer 1 began to orbit Earth in 1958—leading to the discovery of the Van Allen Belts—the see-saw competition between these two major superpowers led to one achievement in space after another, culminating in the Moon landings.

The poems that follow are a partial documentation of the Sputnik-to-Apollo era, a time of many firsts: first man in space, the first space walks, first photos of the Moon's far side, first fly-by of Mars, first probes to crash—then to soft-land—on the Moon. The poems include fetching evocations of childhood memories of the launch of Sputnik and a heart-breaking elegy for Laika, the Soviet dog that was the first animal to orbit Earth, and the first to die in orbit. William Carlos Williams celebrates the first human in space, Yuri Gagarin, while other poets give us the space walks of both the Russian and American programs. Pablo Neruda's poem gestures toward views of the Space Race from countries it was meant to sway, and its inclusion suggests the uncharted scope of global poetic responses. One legacy of this Cold War competition and the potential for it to become hot is eerily portrayed in Loren Eiseley's "Sunset at Laramie." This work reflects America's obsession with a period when the Soviet Union dominated the quest for space and the ongoing competition between the nations.

All along, it seemed clear that both nations—both ideologies—were shooting for the Moon. While the Apollo missions provoked a veritable outpouring of poetry, the first automated probes brought only limited reactions. May Swenson's work is one of the notable among them, including lines that would represent many skeptical writers' viewpoint: "Moon / old fossil / to be scrubbed / and studied / like a turtle's stomach." Mary Ellen Solt, an avant-garde "concrete" or visual poet, takes a more playful approach in her "Moonshot Sonnet," in which lunar probe transmissions are converted to symbols that look like the hieroglyphs of some advanced galactic civilization. Perhaps the most exuberant expression of what space might hold for us in this selection—and perhaps in this anthology as a whole—is British poet Edwin Morgan's "For the International Poetry Incarnation": "Worldscene! Worldtime! Spacebreaker! Wildship! Starman!" This is no Beat irony, as one finds in Allen Ginsburg's "Poem Rocket." Morgan concludes with "Beginning singing, born to go . . ."

This excitement is not reflected in Ronald Duncan's persona poem in which an astronaut admits "I'm a man who was never troubled with any emotion." Emotion matters—but not in a gender-stereotyped way—in Enid Shomer's "A Lady Astronaut Tests for Space," which offers a glimpse into unofficial efforts to consider female candidates for the American space program. That endeavor would be quashed by the U.S. government. The Soviets would get there first, launching Valentina Tereshkova in 1963; the United States wouldn't send a woman to space until Sally Ride twenty years later. The first African American in space was Guy Bluford, also in 1983.

Like the spacefarer's absent feelings in Ronald Duncan's poem, much is missing in the poetic documentation of the

Sputnik-to-Apollo era. No poem commemorating the first woman in space. No scenes from Baikonur. This era is nearly a century old, and the poems here attest to its complicated vibrancy. Other poets may take on missions of returning to this time and exploring so much of what remains to be documented and imagined and reimagined.

After all, wouldn't some of us want to be up there on the Project Manhigh balloon (or a future near-space tourism flight), eating a sandwich and looking through a tiny porthole and seeing the blue curve of Earth? Perhaps a poet will take us there soon, high above and yesterdays ago.

Christopher Cokinos

CORRINNE CLEGG HALES

SPUTNIK: OCTOBER 4, 1957

The day I got my blond hair cut off short like a boy's was the same day
The Russians sent their revolutionary Sputnik into space. The hairdresser
Reached over and turned up the volume on the pale green plastic radio
Sitting on her kitchen counter, and we listened in amazement as she lopped off
Every one of my home-permanent curls. So you want to be a boy,
She'd said, lighting a cigarette and taking a long drag.
What does your mama say? I said it wasn't my mama's hair.
So she held my head under running water in the kitchen sink, handed me
A towel and began to spread newspapers over the shiny linoleum floor.
Then she poured herself a cup of coffee, sat me down on a rolling chair
And started her deliberate combing and cutting. Space extends in all directions
The news voice told us, and has no known limits or outward boundaries.

She talked around her cigarette, dipping her rat-tail comb in a glass of water
And pulling it through my hair repeatedly as she worked. I watched
Myself transform in the narrow framed mirror she propped up against
The wall in front of me. It made us look taller than we were and thin,
And everything in the room—the toaster, the coffee pot,
The copper bottom skillet on the stove—became brighter
And more intense as she combed out each long, separate lock

And cut it free, dropping all that false feminine weight
Piece by piece to the floor. The radio was giving us a lesson:
Escape velocity—To overcome the earth's gravity completely
And reach interplanetary space, a rocket must reach a minimum velocity,
Or speed, of about 25,000 miles an hour. This is about 7 miles a second.
Scientists call this "escape velocity."

I planned to get a paper route and ride fast through the streets
Like my brothers, throwing tightly rolled papers precisely and hard,
Never missing a door. The hairdresser flicked ash into the sink
And said the Russians were going to land on the moon before long. She said
You had to give credit where credit is due; maybe now Uncle Sam would get
His own ass in gear. And then she said the moon is a woman. Just like that.
And the radio went on defining terms: Sputnik is a Russian word
Meaning fellow traveler. The artificial satellite is simply
A man-made moon. She was turning me around in the chair
As she clipped more and more and my hair was falling
Free and light all around me. I repeated: escaping the earth, lunar conquest,
Beyond the moon, speed, weight, burnout, rocket, G-force, orbit, payload,
Probe, propellant, thrust. The words were power on my tongue.

When the hairdresser's hungry cat scratched at the screen door
And we both jumped at the noise, the scissors took a tiny nick
Off the top of my right ear. She stopped, pinched the blood
From my ear and smiled at my face in the mirror. Almost finished,
She slowly navigated the shape of my skull with electric clippers, leaving
An even half inch, then lathered my neck with soap and shaved a straight line
Across the back. See, you're not so different as a boy, she was saying, just
    another
Side of the same shiny coin. I imagined that little Russian moon revolving
Effortlessly above us, above the whole world, and everything
Seemed possible. At the end of our universe, the radio expert said,
Interstellar space begins. Our own galaxy, or star system, ends
At unimaginable distances from the earth. Here, intergalactic space,
Or space between the galaxies, begins and never ends.
The cat was still scratching to get in, and we were two women
Laughing, running our hands over my new prickly hair.

DAVID CLEWELL

UNCLE BUD, UNSHAKEN IN THE WAKE OF *SPUTNIK:* OCTOBER 1957

i.

Maybe because they were strangely so much alike: 180 pounds
and transmitting essentially meaningless signals from their distance—
although *Sputnik*, with its intermittent beeping, was moving undeniably
faster than my uncle, orbiting the Earth every hour-and-a-half.
It took Bud that long just to wake up, make coffee, and scramble his eggs
before heading into another day full of his unfinished, get-rich-quick
inventions, muttering to himself on his unhurried way to anywhere.
Overnight, the Russians had clearly taken most of the world by surprise,
and what, exactly, was that satellite supposed to be doing up there, anyway?
No one ever really knew what Uncle Bud was up to, either,
clanking and banging through so many impossible nights in his workshed,
but they weren't about to lose any real sleep over him.

ii.

The only reason for the beeping: a one-volt-battery-powered radio
   transmitter
so *Sputnik* could be tracked over those three weeks before it fell
silent. It stayed in orbit another seventy days, visible to anyone looking up
just beyond the familiar horizon. And Uncle Bud couldn't help but look

quietly upon it, every chance he got. He saw it as someone's personal triumph, no matter how small—old-fashioned know-how flying high, before the inevitable crash-and-burn.

Half a world away, Little Richard saw it too, during an outdoor concert in Australia, and took it somehow as a sign more divine than ingeniously human. Immediately, he walked off the stage, renounced rock 'n' roll, and for a while fell into his own good-golly brand of evangelism. But Uncle Bud was saying to hell with rock 'n' roll long before *Sputnik* was even a gleam in Little Richard's wide eyes.

iii.

And while the Cold War was taken to new, out-of-this-world heights, the fear was still down-to-earth. The country that had launched this harmless beach ball of a satellite surely wasn't doing it for fun, could just as easily target anywhere on the planet with a guided nuclear warhead. And this was only a guess: that would be us. And so a suddenly white-knuckled USA got cracking. Thanks to those no-goodnik Russians, I'd soon be weighed down with more grade-school science and arithmetic than I'd ever counted on, now that we had serious catching-up to do—even if no one could touch us when it came to engineering the coolest automotive tail fins in the world.

iv.

On the same day that *Sputnik* was fired into orbit—the first in an upcoming flurry of launches we insisted, for a while, on calling *space-shots*— Jimmy Hoffa was elected Teamsters president. He stayed aloft for years before disappearing into the vastness of some different space altogether. *Leave It to Beaver* was just getting off the television ground that night. And the Yankees, the goddamn Yankees, were back again in the World Series, where it would be up to Braves pitcher Lew Burdette, spitball or not, to shut them down and finally out.

In the year of the ill-fated Edsel, which went absolutely nowhere, in the year of the worst flu outbreak since the end of World War I, Americans were also coming down all over with acute *Sputnik*-itis—an unhealthy obsession with Russia's eye-opener. Headlines like RED MOON OVER AMERICA had them knocking back their share of Sputnik Cocktails: two parts vodka, one part sour grapes. They'd lighten up later with Sputnik lamps, Sputnik hairdos,

Sputnik shish kebab. They'd come to say *going Sputnik* for anything
that seemed even the least bit way out there, like Uncle Bud himself,
or like those newly christened *beatniks* that Bud had no time for, either.
But first it was the night-sweats, weakness, a national case
of the willies. Report after unconfirmed report had *Sputnik* setting off
thousands of those new electric garage-door openers all across the country.

v.

Twelve years later, America would finally put its foot down,
beating the Russians to the Moon. Bud would find it tough to believe
anyone was truly on the Moon and not a top-secret movie set hidden away
in Arizona or somewhere else he'd never been. My Uncle Bud—
always one small step or two ahead of his conspiratorial time.
Either way, it was hard to imagine in 1957—not even that much cold comfort
in the shadow of *Sputnik* on those crisp October nights, a long way from any
Sea of Tranquillity, from Armstrong and Aldrin and especially that third guy,
just along for the high-powered ride. The one who'd get stuck with
staying behind, locked into his solitary lunar orbit, no doubt cursing
his short-straw luck—forever miles away from any real historic action.
Of everything NASA would try to sell him, that much, at least, Bud would buy.

vi.

The only beeping I heard was the horn of Bud's worn-out Buick.
From my bedroom window I could see him again, painfully visible
to the naked eye, straining under the weight of whatever he was lifting
this time out of the trunk: a patchwork masterpiece of metal, bulbs, and wires
he began to assemble in the moonlit driveway—two parts Buck Rogers
and one part Sears, Roebuck—taking me into his ridiculous confidence again
because I was the only one in the family who believed in him, or at least
believed in the idea of him: *I've been working on something
that can bring it crashing down.* Uncle Bud had thought it over
and decided, on behalf of the greater good, there was nothing else to be done.
And so there we were, mostly in the dark, aiming his latest contraption
into space, whatever it was, both of us hunkering down in our Cold War
rosebushes bunker, waiting for anything small and brilliant to flash by
over our heads, for the telltale garage door to open for no apparent reason.
But he would know better—and me too, just then, for knowing him.

And when
the motorized garage door actually lifted, we still could hardly believe it:
my mother standing at the switch, awakened from a fitful sleep, not quite
dreaming what was going down that night, right there in her own
American backyard. My uncle and I were no rocket scientists, but
we had a feeling—*Sputnik* or no *Sputnik*—there was going to be trouble
if she spotted us in the bushes among her beloved American Beauties or what
was left of them that late in the year. Those reds and purples: the only
true colors of blood and bruise—as if all the radiant pain of being alive
had come together in a single tight bud, making ready to blossom
into one last, inexplicably joyful noise.

CHRISTOPHER COKINOS

THE NAZIS AT WHITE SANDS

Nice work

if you can get it

—this

dragging

of corpses

to the bench

with only so much

coffee. Harder

still, apogee.

Glamorous

if they think

it's glamorous.

Scary, only in

the old novel sense

and the world knows

which one they mean.

Clamp failing

lunar light

under the instrument

and it still ends up

with Tuesday, faulty

graphite vane before

some ration, cakes of khaki meatloaf

cloud New Mexico blue,

a bent fork behind

a cracked sink, gyros

and ridiculous amounts

of sand. *Frau im Mond*'s

Oberth gleams,

gleams. Captains

lording memos like

gravity itself

were American, geometry

invented by Franklin.

An uncouth Bakelite radio.

They were lovelorn, o

in the barracks

but grateful

. . . 'neath a starry sky . . .

Strikes of the typist

were, in 1944, the only sounds

by six calves of three hanging

requisitions. What dreams,

von Braun, of under

the mountain factory

are this calculus? How

they pleased, the rockets'

rise from Dora, the rockets'

fall on Chiswick, which landed

them blinking in this American desert.

A light breeze still lauds : in black and silver

thread, their insignia.

FRANK PAINO

LAIKA

First dog to be launched into low earth orbit, Sputnik 2,
3 November 1957

Because she'd gone unbroken
by three years on Moscow's barren streets,

she'd proved her will to survive simply
by surviving and so was chosen

for a kind of brute salvation, a halfway gift
whose bad conclusion was already written

in a lack of funds and time and the keen
knowing, like something obscene shouted

through cloister halls, there'd be no way
to take it back. And so began fierce weeks

of acclimation: each cage smaller
than the last to accustom her to stricture,

the relentless gyre of the centrifuge, and
crude machines to simulate the cacophonous dirge

of ignition, shrieking metal, everything
it would take to lift a thirteen-pound mongrel

into history. He called her "Little Curly."
"Little Bug." As if naming the doomed,

taking her home one night to play
with his two bright-eyed daughters,

could make the great burden of her death
a lighter thing to bend beneath

when it came time to tighten the harness
just once again and no more,

to hold her in waiting three restless days
within that aluminum tomb

where she could stand or lie but never turn,
and late October's chill settled its silver pall

while the red-lit counter counted
down. Three days and, finally, ascent—

three anxious hours back on Earth
before they saw her heart's green tracery

slow again to nearly calm
while the unshed core quietly kindled

its black wick inside the polished dome.
Listen, there is no other way to tell a thing

that has no mercy in it:
she burned up from the inside.

Fevered. Frantic. Blood-boiled.
Six hundred miles between herself and

solid ground.
And there's no faith to be placed

in the weary myth of sacrifice;
no way to make right

the trust that was betrayed—
the muzzle and fragrant paws

and mad tongue of it—
how she was thrust into weightlessness,

into the useless memory of
steady hands, of the man who

spoke softly, who turned, at last,
from the wild extravagance

of the round and riveted window
about which he'd been so adamant,

as if she might somehow savor
the breathless view, the spinning blue

that beckoned like a ball tossed into a street
she could only return to in flames.

WILLIAM CARLOS WILLIAMS

HEEL & TOE TO THE END

Gagarin says, in ecstasy,
he could have
gone on forever

he floated
ate and sang
and when he emerged from that

one hundred eight minutes off
the surface of
the earth he was smiling

Then he returned
to take his place
among the rest of us

from all that division and
subtraction a measure
toe and heel

heel and toe he felt
as if he had
been dancing

ENID SHOMER

A LADY ASTRONAUT TESTS FOR SPACE

Secret women's Mercury Project,
Albuquerque, New Mexico, 1961

Science is good to a point, but how do you measure
guts? Can numbers predict who'd dive through a fire
to rescue a child? How will you gauge bravery?
By dexterity, stamina, reflexes? They aren't the heart
of the matter. I passed the extraocular balance test.
In the Slow Rotating Room they thought I'd launch

my lunch, but a day's fast left nothing to launch.
Strapped to the tilt table, my muscles measured
in ergs, I aced the pressor-reflex test.
I adapted to bright and black light, to fiery
red. If velocity of the ulnar nerve is where heart
resides, then from wrist to elbow I am brave.

While I dreamed of headlines—"NASA Braves
Public Opinion . . . Picks Dame for Space"—they launched
probes into my nose and throat. Heart
pounding, I rode the Dilbert Dunker and measured
up: underwater and upside down, I fired
like a sparkplug and kicked to the surface. For the test

that mimics g-forces, they rigged a test
ejection seat to slide on a vertical track. I braved
the kick of a fifty caliber shell firing
beneath me like a rocket. They say a real launch
feels like a kick in the pants from an immeasurably
larger boot. Last came the heart

exam, the Lee and Gimlette procedure. The heartier
you are, the slower your pulse under stress. The test
discovers leaks in the chamber walls by measuring
blood flow. I've often used bull and bravado
to mask my flaws, but a blaze in my chest nearly launched
me off the table. I turned fishbelly white. Fired

into space, I'd never survive, they said, my fire
doused in the thrust and rattle of gravity's waves. My heart
line on the EKG still spiking like flames, I launched
the excuse that I hadn't been sleeping. It didn't fly. Test
me again, I begged, or let it pass. A life of bravery
should outweigh a single graph. Here's the measure

of my mettle, what testing can't reveal: launched
on a column of fire into measureless space, I'd brave the dark
heart of creation. I don't care if I never get back.

PABLO NERUDA
TRANSLATED BY FORREST GANDER

21

Those two solitary men,
those first men
up there,
what of ours did they
bring with them?
What from us, the men
of Earth?

It occurs to me
that the light was fresh then,
that an unwinking star
journeyed along
cutting short and linking
distances,
their faces unused
to the awesome desolation,
in pure space
among astral bodies polished and glistening
like grass at dawn,
something new came from the earth,
wings or bone-coldness,
enormous drops of water

or surprise
thoughts, a strange bird
throbbing
to the distant human heart.

And not only that,
but cities, smoke,
the roar of crowds,
bells and violins,
the feet of children leaving school,
all of that is alive
in space now,
from now on,
because the astronauts
didn't go by themselves,
they brought our earth,
the odors of moss and forest,
love, the crisscrossed limbs of men and women,
terrestrial rains over the prairies,
something floated up like
a wedding dress
behind the two spaceships:
it was spring on earth
blooming for the first time
that conquered an inanimate heaven,
depositing in those altitudes
the seed
of our kind.

Refers to the dual flights of USSR's Vostok-3 and -4 in August 1962, the first instance of two manned spacecraft in orbit at the same time. In a 1962 article touching on the same topic, Neruda wrote that "poetry must search for new words to talk about these things. . . . Those two astronauts who communicate with one another, who are watched over and directed from our distant planet, who eat and sleep in the unmapped cosmos, are the poet-discoverers of the world." (El Siglo, Santiago, Chile, August 18, 1962, translated from the Spanish by Lizzie Davis in Then Come Back: The Lost Neruda Poems, *Copper Canyon Press, 2016)*

MARY ELLEN SOLT

MOONSHOT SONNET

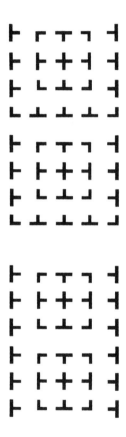

Author's note: *Made by copying the scientists' symbols on the first photos of the moon in the* New York Times: *there were exactly fourteen "lines" with five "accents." We have not been able to address the moon in a sonnet successfully since the Renaissance. Admitting its new scientific content made it possible to do so again. The poem dates from 1964. Drawn by Timothy Mayer. (From* Concrete Poetry: A World View, *Indiana University Press, 1968)*

MAY SWENSON

AFTER THE FLIGHT OF RANGER VII

Moon
old fossil
to be scrubbed
and studied
like a turtle's stomach

prodded over on your back
Invulnerable hump
that stumped us

pincers prepare to
pick your secrets
bludgeons of light
to force your seams

Old fossil
glistening
in the continuous rain
of meteorites
blown to you from

between the stars
Stilt feet
mobilize to alight upon you
Ticking feelers
determine your fissures

to impact a pest
of electric eggs in the
cracks of your cold
volcanoes
Tycho Copernicus Kepler
look for geysers

strange abrasions
zodiacal wounds

LOREN EISELEY

SUNSET AT LARAMIE

Somewhere beyond Laramie the winding freights
still howl their lonesome message to the dark,
the mountain men lie quiet, wolves are gone,
stars circle overhead, huge missiles lie
scattered in firing pens. Computers watch
with radar eyes pinpointed latitudes.
Gigantic cupped ears listen everywhere—
a bear asleep beneath a winter drift,
his pulse is coded, too; night-flying geese
blip by upon horizon screens, slowly we draw a net
converging to ourselves. How strange to hear
trains hoot in blizzards, cattle bawl in cars,
think of the Chisholm trail a century gone, and know
beyond the polar circle other ears now listen.
This daft and troubled century spies and spies,
counts bears' heartbeats, whales' frantic twists and turns.
The background noise of continents drifts in,
captured by satellites. Still far up in the crags
sure-footed mountain sheep climb higher, lift horned heads,
see the night fall below them, hear the train, and stamp
as rams stamp, vaguely troubled, while the glow
on the last peak fades out. Far off a coyote cries,
not in wild darkness, but a haunted night
filled with the turning of vast ears and eyes.

RONALD DUNCAN

FROM *MAN*

Part IV, Canto 3

It's not easy for me to tell you my feelings on that occasion.
I'm a man who was never troubled with any emotions
Particularly deep, as you might say.
That's why they selected me, I suppose.
They didn't want a neurotic, complicated guy,
Whose imagination might upset their calculations;
But somebody physically fit, technically able,
And in control.
Let me put it this way: my nervous system
was unlikely to short-circuit;
They didn't want a guy like you
Who might see some internal vision up there,
then forget to fire the retro-rocket: no offence of course . . .
The psycho-boys screened me for hours:
They said my normality was almost abnormal.
I suppose what they were looking for was somebody
whose emotional attachments were sufficient
to give him the will to live,
but insufficient to cause him to do anything foolish.
Yes, as you say, somebody who was unlikely to over compensate
with an emotional gesture, commit hari-kari,
copulate with the universe or indulge in self-crucifixion,
whatever that is.

And as you suppose, they enquired pretty deeply into my private life:
asked me about my feelings for my mother, my wife and kids
and whether I had any attachment to anybody, on the side.
They seemed pretty satisfied that none of this
Had fouled me up.
And of course, they asked me about my dreams.
I found this pretty embarrassing,
And they seemed pleased that I was embarrassed.
You see, they didn't want a guy
That was introspective or as complicated as a computer in himself
  And certainly nobody who had any spiritual dilemmas.
I must say I got a clean sheet there.
There were questions I'd never considered
  so there were no problems you might say.
They asked me what I believed in and eventually
  I came up with: evolution and efficiency.
Yes. You find that hard to believe? That's how I am.
  Lift-off itself provided no new sensations,
We had gone through the drill too often
  and simulated every detail:
I found it hard to realize this was the real thing.
I remember noticing that the shape of the capsule
        reminded me of something but I couldn't think what,
Until I was strapped in, waiting for the count down,
  And, at the instant of blast off, I realized what it was:
        the exterior of the capsule was the shape of a
          cathode ray tube
And this, I suppose, made me wonder what the inside was like
  The first image was an easter egg.
And then a line of poetry came into my mind—
        God knows from where:
  'Like a worm in the bud.' I nearly said it aloud.
That would have surprised them . . .
  But that was it. There was not time for any other thoughts.
Alone up there you're about as alone
  as a telephone operator
With the whole world talking to you;

They even know your pulse rate,
And when you ought to make water.
  Sure.
And being in orbit gave me no new sensations either.
  You see, we'd been through it all before,
Down here in that gadget
  Which even has a revolving globe outside the porthole.
And of course you get no sense of speed,
  less than on a subway.
You are static, suspended, watching the earth turn round
  like an old cart wheel.
And you're kept busy, very:
      recording, checking, talking back
  to a computer, programming your position,
And fuel consumption: so busy, that sleep
  is the one compelling need up there;
Sleep, where your dreams alone are heavy.
Weightlessness is a wag: Puck, as you might say,
  always up to some joke or tease
taking you unawares. Like when I coughed
  And moved into my own spit getting an eyeful,
getting my own back . . . or the crumbs
which refuse to drop.
But there was nothing new up there,
  leastways not till I opened the hatch
and took that brief walk with my rocket gun . . .
  It's something I didn't tell them,
Something I kept to myself,
      it had no scientific significance
Maybe even you will laugh at me
No, it wasn't fear. I would have told them that;
  But it wasn't fear, I had nothing to fear:
The capsule only forty feet away;
  My oxygen line, straight and not fouled up;
And below me: the earth turning so gently
  trailing its shawl of clouds;
And as I watched it, I felt an emotion so strong

the tears spurted from my eyes.
It wasn't homesickness, but earthsickness;
  A yearning, like a tide inside of me;
I would have swopped the whole universe
  for any foothold on that ball of dirt
Which I wanted then, and loved
  more than I've ever wanted or loved a woman;
I desired the earth, not any part nor any person,
  But it, where I belonged: the whole was home to me.
I guess I was the first man—
  for you can't count Him as one, I suppose?—
to feel such tenderness for the whole damn place
  and any bastard on it.
No, I don't feel it any more. Well, not so intensely.
  Maybe you have to be cut off to be in contact?
Or, maybe, it's only when the body has no weight
  that love becomes the one imponderable?
But, as I say, I didn't tell them about it.

RAYMOND WILSON

SPACE WALK

A nonsense term. To walk
needs feet with something solid
under, the tug at heel
and toe of gravity,
a firmness for the tensed foot's
arch to grope, grip like a ladder's
rungs under it, and hold,
haul, heave against.

      Swimming's
not absolutely the word
either, though what you move through
is suffocating ocean
everywhere, a Dead Sea
noiselessly drowning in
a shoreless flood the whole
of Time.

   We step to walk,
of course. But equally
are said to step into the sea.

JOHN FAIRFAX

ORBITING ARK

120 frogs eggs and 64 blue spiderwort
were launched into earth orbit
in biosatellite 2.

The pepper seed in my pepper mill
favours adventure
knowing now that pepper grows
more quickly in the denser air
than it does on earth.
Flour beetles swell with cunning
pride having spun from Cape Kennedy
in the same satellite as wheat seedlings.
And have you noticed that wasps
are more purposeful this year?

The vinegar gnat abuzz in orbit
leaves the world a lesser place.
And the trip of endless bacteria
makes running noses astroprobe.
Bread and fishes weren't forgotten

10 million spore of orange bread mould
and floating amoebae
lived by a sea of strontium:
but the whole ark returned
to an insane dust man
who plans to make heaven
the same as earth.

One day a planetrider
might hear a plaintive croak
of a bullfrog
and imagine that the blue spiderwort
is spinning webs as quickly
as the capsule
in which he is incubating.

NASA's biosatellite program launched three satellites between 1966 and 1969 to study the effects of spaceflight on biological organisms. Biosatellites 1 and 2 carried insects, frog eggs, plants, and microorganisms. Biosatellite 3 carried a male pig-tailed macaque named Bonnie, who died shortly after the satellite returned to Earth.

ALLEN GINSBERG

POEM ROCKET

"Be a Star-screwer!"
—GREGORY CORSO

Old moon my eyes are new moon with human footprint
no longer Romeo Sadface in drunken river Loony Pierre eyebrow, goof moon
O possible moon in Heaven we get to first of ageless constellations of names
as God is possible as All is possible so we'll reach another life.

Moon politicians earth weeping and warring in eternity

tho not one star disturbed by screaming madmen from Hollywood
oil tycoons from Romania making secret deals with flabby green
    Plutonians—
slave camps on Saturn Cuban revolutions on Mars?
Old life and new side by side, will Catholic church find Christ on Jupiter
Mohammed rave in Uranus will Buddha be acceptable on the stolid planets
or will we find Zoroastrian temples flowering on Neptune?
What monstrous new ecclesiastical designs on the entire universe unfold in
    the dying Pope's brain?
Scientist alone is true poet he gives us the moon
he promises the stars he'll make us a new universe if it comes to that
O Einstein I should have sent you my flaming mss.
O Einstein I should have pilgrimaged to your white hair!

O fellow travellers I write you a poem in Amsterdam in the Cosmos
where Spinoza ground his magic lenses long ago
I write you a poem long ago
already my feet are washed in death
Here I am naked without identity
with no more body than the fine black tracery of pen mark on soft paper
as star talks to star multiple beams of sunlight all the same myriad thought
in one fold of the universe where Whitman was
and Blake and Shelley saw Milton dwelling as in a starry temple
brooding in his blindness seeing all—
Now at last I can speak to you beloved brothers of an unknown moon
real Yous squatting in whatever form amidst Platonic Vapors of Eternity
I am another Star.
Will you eat my poems or read them
or gaze with aluminum blind plates on sunless pages?
do you dream or translate & accept data with indifferent droopings of antennae?
do I make sense to your flowery green receptor eyesockets? do you have
    visions of God?
Which way will the sunflower turn surrounded by millions of suns?

This is my rocket my personal rocket I send up my message Beyond
Someone to hear me there
My immortality
without steel or cobalt basalt or diamond gold or mercurial fire
without passports filing cabinets bits of paper warheads
without myself finally
pure thought
message all and everywhere the same
I send up my rocket to land on whatever planet awaits it
preferably religious sweet planets no money
fourth dimensional planets where Death shows movies
plants speak (courteously) of ancient physics and poetry itself is manufac-
    tured by the trees
the final Planet where the Great Brain of the Universe sits waiting for a poem
    to land in His golden pocket
joining the other notes mash-notes love-sighs complaints-musical shrieks of
    despair and the million unutterable thoughts of frogs

I send you my rocket of amazing chemical
more than my hair my sperm or the cells of my body
the speeding thought that flies upward with my desire as instantaneous as
   the universe and faster than light
and leave all other questions unfinished for the moment to turn back to sleep
   in my dark bed on earth.

EDWIN MORGAN

FOR THE INTERNATIONAL POETRY INCARNATION

Royal Albert Hall, 11 June 1965

Worldscene! Worldtime! Spacebreaker! Wildship! Starman!
Gemini man dangles white and golden—the world floats
on a gold cord and curves blue white beautiful below him—
Vostok shrieks and prophesies, Mariner's prongs flash—
to the wailing of Voskhod Earth sighs, she shakes men loose at last—
out, in our time, to be living seeds sent far beyond
even imagination, though imagination is awake—take
poets on your voyages! Prometheus
embraces Icarus and in a gold shell with wings
he launches him up through the ghostly detritus
of gods and dirty empires and dying laws,
he mounts, he cries, he shouts, he shines, he streams
like light new done, his home is in a sun
and he shall be the burning unburned one.
In darkness, Daedalus
embraces Orpheus, the dark lips caked with earth and roots
he kisses open, the cold body he rubs
to a new life—the dream
flutters in a cage of crumbling bars, reviving

and then beginning slowly singing of the stars.

Beginning singing, born to go.
To cut the cord of gold. To get
the man new born to go.

APOLLO

AS WITH newspapers around the world, the *New York Times* covered the July 20, 1969, Apollo 11 Moon landing with photographs, huge headlines, and articles. But the *Times* also commemorated the landing in unique fashion with a front-page poem. It was not the first time the paper of record had turned to literature to mark such a milestone. Just months before, also on page one, there appeared an essay about the Apollo 8 flight, the first to reach the Moon in orbit, though not to land. In both cases, the author was the patrician man of letters, poet and public servant Archibald MacLeish.

In his poem "Voyage to the Moon," what was formerly a "silver evasion in our farthest thought" and "a wonder to us, unattainable" has now had its surface visited by humans for the first time. The poem has the flavor of an epic: "three days and three nights we journeyed" through a vast distance and even "crossed the invisible tide-rip where the floating dust / falls one way or the other in the void between," an image of moving from the gravity well of Earth to that of the Moon. The language invokes the sublime—the encounter with grandeur that could kill but that does not, that, instead, leaves us in awe. The astronauts "set foot at last upon her beaches," a rhythmic phrase that recalls the Moon's folkloric associations with moisture and how we once thought the Moon might have in fact "maria" or seas of actual water rather than solidified lava. In the end, the astronauts look at Earth as we have looked at the Moon, seeking "a meaning to us, / O, a meaning!"

"Voyage to the Moon" is certainly one of the most widely read serious literary poems on initial publication, on the day after the Moon landing. Nearly a million people saw MacLeish's work, a figure eclipsed perhaps only by the Apollo poems that James Dickey published in *Life* magazine, with its several million readers. Dickey also read his poem "The Moon Ground" on ABC News Apollo 11 coverage, which can be found online. His poem provides a sober counterpart to MacLeish's praiseful tone. Less well-known was John William Andrews's *A.D. Twenty-One Hundred: A Narrative of Space*, which used insistent rhyming quatrains to exuberantly record the early space age and imagine its future.

Such optimism was an outlier in American poetry's response to Apollo. Still under the sway of a Romantic conception of the human mechanized sullying of nature and a Modernist sense of fragmentation, irony, and technological doubt, most poets writing in English reacted to lunar exploration with notes of hesitation if not outright disdain. They included in their stanzas references to the Moon's mythological and symbolic existence for so much of human history, an existence now stained, they thought, by Apollo's technological achievement and its only partial scientific justification. The reason for the program was of course largely geopolitical—a clear race to win prestige at home and around the world by beating the Soviet Union to that stark, gray surface, that "magnificent desolation," as Apollo 11 moonwalker Buzz Aldrin put it. The military connotations, despite the "we came in peace for all mankind" lunar lander plaque, were certainly on the minds of many poets responding to Apollo. Editors and critics Laurence Goldstein, Ronald Weber, and Karen Yelena Olsen, among others, have discussed these matters.

In the following selection, readers will find that, among others, W. H. Auden and Campbell McGrath heaped scorn on Apollo. Lisel Mueller structures her poem with a series of farewells to the

Moon we once knew and ends with a "scarface hello." Anne Sexton, prominent among feminist responders to the Apollo landings, adopted the voice of the Moon itself, saying that the astronauts "walk into me like a barracks . . . / you of the blast off, / you of the bastion, / you of the scheme." But other poets, including more recent ones, have taken other approaches. Patricia Smith remembers how her mother doubted the landings took place, while Gabrielle Calvocoressi recalls a childhood longing to escape and soar with Captain Jim Lovell. In this section, we are fortunate to have poems that reference the African American women "calculators" made famous in the book and film *Hidden Figures* and the seamstresses who crafted space suits. Bruce Bond writes an elegy for the last man to walk on the Moon, Gene Cernan, while among the poets contemporary with the first Apollo flights, Robert Hayden struck a characteristically reflective tone: "What do we ask of these men? / What do we ask of ourselves?"

Hayden's ambivalence was also shared by the public. In 1949, Gallup polling found strong majorities expected cancer cures and nuclear aircraft and trains in the next half-century. Just fifteen percent expected a flight to the moon by 1999. This number grew in the following decade. The year 1950 saw the release of the film *Destination Moon*, and the fifties were marked by science-fiction and science-fact efforts to popularize space exploration, including shows produced by Walt Disney and articles and spreads in influential publications such as *Collier's*. There was never an overwhelming and sustained strong majority in favor of the Moon flights. In 1969, by the time two missions had orbited the Moon and one had landed, public opinion was against moving on to Mars, and some 40 percent wanted NASA's funding cut.

The tumult of the 1960s was a crucial context for Apollo and part of its undoing. This was the era of the Bay of Pigs disaster, the Cuban Missile Crisis and continuing threats of mutually assured nuclear destruction, John F. Kennedy's assassination, proxy conflicts including the grinding and controversial Vietnam War, street protests against the same, the burgeoning Civil Rights Movement, the rise of feminism, and the transformation of America's lands conservation movement to a wider kind of environmentalism.

Apollo was for many a light of optimism, no matter one's attitudes to these momentous events and changes. A prime example of what historian David Nye and others call the technological sublime, the lunar flights were a point of pride for millions of Americans. This had a nationalist tinge, of course, but it also pointed to what sociologist William Sims Bainbridge has called "space idealism," a sense that in going to space we expand our knowledge, help ensure a longer life span for our and other species, and gain a larger, more tender perspective on our home world. The flight of Apollo 8, with its famous Earthrise photo and the recitation of the opening lines of Genesis, at the end of 1968—a year marked by the assassinations of Martin Luther King Jr. and Robert Kennedy—seemed to offer some counterpoint. Indeed, many credit photos of Earth taken from space and the Moon as vital to growing environmental awareness.

The sheer audacity of the program remains astounding. President Kennedy announced the goal of "landing a man on the Moon and returning him safely to the Earth" by 1970 before we had even orbited an astronaut. The program moved quickly from the one-man Mercury missions (all men, yes, despite William Randolph Lovelace's unofficial Woman in Space Program) to the two-man Gemini missions that perfected such activities as space walks and orbital rendezvous to the Apollo missions that forged ahead after the tragic death of the Apollo 1 astronauts in a launch-pad training fire. The total cost was some $24 billion in its day or about $150 billion in more recent valuations. (By comparison, the second U.S. war in Iraq cost nearly $2.5 trillion.) The program's technological benefits remain somewhat controversial—we could argue about Velcro now—but Apollo and the robotic probes that preceded it cast scientific light on our nearest celestial neighbor and showed us that we could reach other worlds. Quite recently, new techniques used on Moon rocks returned by the astronauts have shown that water is locked inside them, a stunning reversal of the paradigm of a bone-dry Moon.

As we gain distance from the Apollo era, there seems to be a renewed appreciation for the feat of landing humans on the Moon and what it tells us about our aspirations for an uncertain future.

Perhaps this derives from our sense of growing fragility in what has been called the Anthropocene, the geologic age of Earth in which humans have so altered its surface and atmosphere that the continued vibrancy of the biosphere and indeed our own species' survival is at stake. With the discovery of water ice in permanently shadowed areas at the lunar poles and with an energetic private sector determined to reach the Moon and Mars, we can remember the Apollo era not only with nostalgia and ambivalence but with a standpoint that holds them both together. Along that line, like the terminator that divides the lunar night and day, we can walk and appreciate both paradox and promise.

The imagery of the lunar surface, the moments of drama, the increasing understanding of the science of the Moon and that it retains mysteries—all of this, as we will see in later sections, portends among some poets a more sympathetic stance not only toward past lunar exploration but toward the possible, if just partial, human future in outer space. It was the seeking of a unity of human purpose on Earth and in space that was behind a much-forgotten part of one mission. On the Apollo 15 orbits around the Moon, Command Module Pilot Al Worden would greet Earth each time he returned from the far side and reestablished radio contact; he did so in ten different languages. While many Apollo astronauts wrote nonfiction accounts—the most notable being Michael Collins's *Carrying the Fire*—Worden first turned to poetry, publishing *Hello Earth* in 1974. It documents his experiences from training to return. In his poem "Oceans," he deploys description and rhyme to capture the pre-launch beauty of the Florida landscape. He ends with a question: "Could it be a Lunar flight / Is one small step towards home?" Worden has the distinction of being the most isolated human being in history. His orbit took him 2,235 miles from his surface compatriots, James Irwin and Dave Scott. To convey that lunar and celestial sublime, to speak out of that void, he turned to poetry.

There are many gaps in the poetic documentation of the Apollo era; like other art forms, poetry about it has reflected primarily an interest in the astronauts and the landings. Part of that interest has included a focus on what author Frank White terms "the overview effect"—a sense of Earth's isolation and beauty and the need both for homely stewardship and cosmic travel. Many in today's public have experienced versions of this feeling virtually, through science-fictional imagery and real astronomical views. Perhaps too they feel it in poems, including and beyond the skepticism of many poets during the time of Apollo. There are poets coming back to the Moon landings with other perspectives. All these words testify to the era, its legacy, and what it tells us about ourselves.

Christopher Cokinos

MAY SWENSON

LANDING ON THE MOON

When in the mask of night there shone that cut,
we were riddled. A probe reached down
and stroked some nerve in us,
as if the glint from a wizard's eye, of silver,
slanted out of the mask of the unknown—
pit of riddles, the scratch-marked sky.

When, albino bowl on cloth of jet,
it spilled its virile rays,
our eyes enlarged, our blood reared with the waves.
We craved its secret, but unreachable
it held away from us, chilly and frail.
Distance kept it magnate. Enigma made it white.

When we learned to read it with our rod,
reflected light revealed
a lead mirror, a bruised shield
seamed with scars and shadow-soiled.
A half-faced sycophant, its glitter borrowed,
rode around our throne.

On the moon there shines earth light
as moonlight shines upon the earth . . .
If on its obsidian we set our weightless foot,
and sniff no wind, and lick no rain
and feel no gauze between us and the Fire,
will we trot its grassless skull, sick for the homelike shade?

Naked to the earth-beam we will be,
who have arrived to map an apparition,
who walk upon the forehead of a myth.
Can flesh rub with symbol? If our ball
be iron, and not light, our earliest wish
eclipses. Dare we land upon a dream?

MARY ELLEN SOLT

ELEGY FOR THREE ASTRONAUTS

```
              w   w   w

              i   i   i

              d   d   d

a  s  t  r              n  a  u  t

a  s  t  r      O       n  a  u  t

a  s  t  r              n  a  u  t

              w   w   w

              i   i   i

              d   d   d

              o   o   o

              w   w   w
```

astronaut
satronau
starona
staron
staro
star
stars
starsa
starsai
starsail
starsailo
starsailor

starsailor
satrsailo
astrsao
astrso
astro
astron
astrona
astronau
astronaut

astronaut
satronau
starona
staron
staro
star
stars
starsa
starsai
starsail
starsailo
starsailor

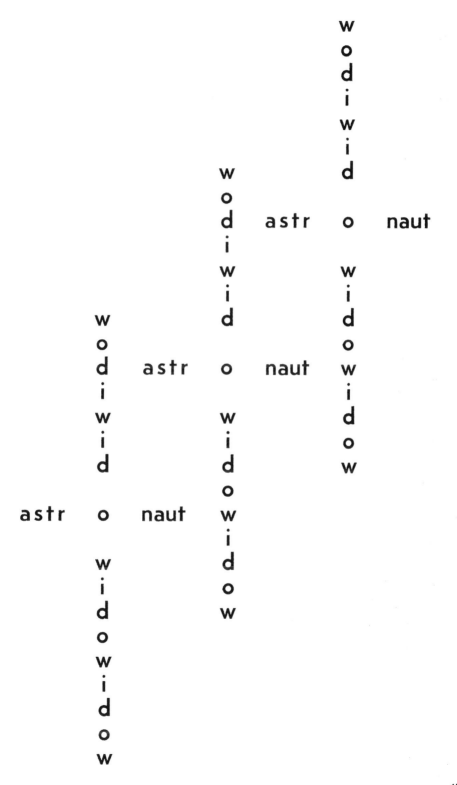

JESSE DE ANGELIS

AMERICAN SPACESUIT

For Hazel Fellows

In this room, the Singers are always running
through a man's shape, thread in lockstitch.

Someone is always here, working.
Julia dips the shells in latex, Velma glues

the layers of Mylar together. I sew.
Today is the part that touches skin,

that lets his own heat warm him. My needle's
the only thing that gets so close.

/

It's a job, no one's dream. Later, I'll see him
on the TV, floating naked and warm

inside what I made for him. We never saw
the faces. I read his measurements off a card.

/

This plant used to make underwear,
smaller, softer things. We cut, we sewed. We knew

all the shapes a body could be made to take.
There are only some things fabric won't do.

/

The first day we switched to space, the bosses
called us all over. Said we'd have to learn

it all again, like a second first time.
They took my pins,

doled them out slow. Just the thinnest layer
between this and nothing.

/

But we already knew the job:
how to hold the thread, the way the layers

lap over one another, every way the suit
would float and hang. They listened to our scissors,

to the needle pushing through. When we knew
how not to follow them, the patterns changed

without thanks. I already knew
the ways cloth can keep a body safe.

/

If they found a stray pin,
they'd press it into your skin.

/

When the suit was all shaped and layered,
when it looked like the man, white

and headless on the worktable,
we sent him off.

He came back wearing a little card
saying where he didn't fit. I spent days

slicing apart each stitch, unpiecing
everything I'd made around him.

/

We began it again—the machines had run
too fast. The needles eating through him,

fabric pulled wrong. For each inch of flex,
a hundred hours of my back, bent.

Swapped out the treadles;
each stitch another footfall.

Yes, he'll fly. First, we'll walk
the whole way out for him.

/

And what I'm still doing is sitting
in a white room in Dover, Delaware.

Hundreds of hands are passing his form
back and forth under the banks of fluorescents.

I'm feeding his fabric into my machine,
thinking about the easy way smoke

could be rising from a cigarette's lit tip.
How, in rising, it becomes nothing.

ELAINE V. EMANS

THE CREW OF *APOLLO 8*

Shall we call them poets, for having observed
on their earliest times around
the moon that it seemed to be
layered with
a grayish white beach sand
with footprints in it? Or geologists
for having reported to us
the six or seven terraces leading
down
into crater Langrenus?

Or shall we call them some new
breed of bird
for having swiftly flown
weightless and unfearing and
sharp-eyed
into the dark unknown?
Yet words to tell of their skill and
valiancy
are as weak as water—
and their return, and being earthlings
with us
again, are what most matter.

X . J . K E N N E D Y

SPACE

for Martin Green

I

Who could have thought, but for eight days in space,
The heart might learn to thrive on weightlessness,
As though with no flesh holding it in place,
Yearning by choice, not made to by distress,
Turning in free fall on reprieve from earth
We tug-of-war with daily for the sakes
Of those we long for, those we help bring forth.
How will it be when all the strength it takes
To rip moons loose from planet boughs, or send
Engines of slag careening from their track
Into the unending dark, end over slow end,
Is in the twist that opens a door a crack?
Who will need long to savor his desire
When wishes no more blunt them against bulk,
But pierce straight through; when acts, once dreamt, transpire?
Man may imagine man's own mother's milk.

II

Heads bowed in fetal crouch, the Gemini
Float in their pear-shaped comfort. Data grows
By little clicks, as pine cones, drying free
And dropping, pile up. Enter, through a hose,

Essence of roast beef. Signs that flash ABORT
Bespeak a tube's break. If all hold, instead,
The moon's thin skin shall cringe under their boots—
Just as we always thought, the thing's stone dead.

III

Hope to be disembodied reconciles
Our drifted hearts to that exacting beat.
We clerks-without-church look on while slide-rules
Render our lusts and madnesses concrete.
It may well be that when I rev my car
And let it overtake and pass my thinking,
It's space I crave; when my electric bar
Sets up a moonshot, lemon-oiled and clinking,
And gulp by gulp, I shrug the world's dull weight,
Out after what I had long thought I'd hate.

ARCHIBALD MACLEISH

VOYAGE TO THE MOON

Wanderer in our skies,
dazzle of silver in our leaves and on our
waters silver, O
silver evasion in our farthest thought—
"the visiting moon," "the glimpses of the moon,"

and we have found her.

　　　　　　　　From the first of time,
before the first of time, before the
first men tasted time, we sought for her.
She was a wonder to us, unattainable,
a longing past the reach of longing,
a light beyond our lights, our lives—perhaps
a meaning to us—O, a meaning!

Now we have found her in her nest of night.

Three days and three nights we journeyed,
steered by farthest stars, climbed outward,

crossed the invisible tide-rip where the floating dust
falls one way or the other in the void between,
followed that other down, encountered
cold, faced death, unfathomable emptiness.

Now, the fourth day evening, we descend,
make fast, set foot at last upon her beaches,
stand in her silence, lift our heads and see
above her, wanderer in her sky,
a wonder to us past the reach of wonder,
a light beyond our lights, our lives, the rising
earth,

      a meaning to us,

             O, a meaning!

N. SCOTT MOMADAY

WALK ON THE MOON

For Henry Raymont

21 July 1969

Extend, there where you venture and come back,
The edge of Time. Be it your farthest track.
Time in that distance wanes. What is *to be*,
That present verb, there in Tranquility?

D. M. THOMAS

FROM "COMPUTER 70: DREAMS & LOVEPOEMS"

4

I walked upon that lunar sea,
a second Adam to the flood;
the desert called Tranquillity
battered with meteorites. I stood,

as in Korea or Vietnam.
A barren plain that's drunk its gore.
In heaven too, I saw, the Ram
is slaughtered in a slower war.

Seconal was my only peace,
patented on our own dark star;
oxygen was love; to find out this,
strange, that I had to fly so far.

Unfiltered the sun's furnace roared;
a shadow was its fierce extreme;
a saviour round my body poured
cool water of Siloah's stream.

Even as the fish who rose to us
bore its own sea into our veins,
if we embrace the universe,
we must bring trees, we must bring rains.

We must bring dreams. I walked on ground
not sanctified by joy or sin.
Dream-emptiness stretched all around.
I wondered when life would begin.

Each second crammed with robot task;
EVA, the shadow I pursued;
tried to shut out, behind my mask,
the solitude's deeper solitude.

My rib in pain, as though some Eve
would spring, I slept but fitfully.
I felt it sad that I must leave
only my footprints on the sea.

ROBERT HAYDEN

ASTRONAUTS

Armored in oxygen,
        faceless in visors—
mirrormasks reflecting
        the mineral glare and
shadow of moonscape—
        they walk slowmotion
floatingly the lifeless
        dust of Taurus
Littrow. And Wow, they
        exclaim; oh boy, this is it.

        They sing, exulting
(though trained to be wary
        of "emotion and
philosophy"), breaking
        the calcined stillness
of once Absolute Otherwhere.

Risking edges, earthlings
        to whom only
their machines are friendly
        (and God's radar-
watching eye?), they
        labor at gathering
proof of hypothesis;
        in snowshine of sunlight
dangerous as radium
        probe detritus for clues.

        What is it we wish them
to find for us, as
        we watch them on our
screens? They loom there
        heroic antiheroes,
smaller than myth and
        poignantly human.
Why are we troubled?
        What do we ask of these men?
What do we ask of ourselves?

STANLEY KUNITZ

THE FLIGHT OF APOLLO

1

Earth was my home, but even there I was a stranger. This mineral crust. I walk like a swimmer. What titanic bombardments in those old astral wars! I know what I know: I shall never escape from strangeness or complete my journey. Think of me as nostalgic, afraid, exalted. I am your man on the moon, a speck of megalomania, restless for the leap toward island universes pulsing beyond where the constellations set. Infinite space overwhelms the human heart, but in the middle of nowhere life inexorably calls to life. Forward my mail to Mars. What news from the Great Spiral Nebula in Andromeda and the Magellanic Clouds?

2

I was a stranger on earth.
Stepping on the moon, I begin
the gay pilgrimage to new
Jerusalems
in foreign galaxies.
Heat. Cold. Craters of silence.
The Sea of Tranquility
rolling on the shores of entropy.
And, beyond,
the intelligence of the stars.

LISEL MUELLER

A FAREWELL, A WELCOME

After the lunar landings

Good-bye pale cold inconstant
tease, you never existed
therefore we had to invent you

    Good-bye crooked little man
    huntress who sleeps alone
    dear pastor, shepherd of stars
    who tucked us in   Good-bye

Good riddance phony prop
con man moon
who tap-danced with June
to the tender surrender
of love from above

Good-bye decanter of magic liquids
fortuneteller *par excellence*
seducer   incubus   medicine man
exile's sanity   love's sealed lips
womb that nourished the monstrous child

and the sweet ripe grain   Good-bye
      We trade you in as we traded
      the evil eye for the virus
      the rosy seat of affections
      for the indispensable pump
we say good-bye as we said good-bye
to angels in nightgowns   to Grandfather God

Good-bye forever Edam and Gorgonzola
cantaloupe in the sky
night watchman, one-eyed loner
wolves   nevertheless
are programmed to howl   Good-bye
      forbidden lover good-bye
      sleepwalkers will wander
      with outstretched arms for no reason
      while you continue routinely
      to husband the sea, prevail
      in the fix of infant strabismus
Good-bye ripe ovum   women will spill their blood
in spite of you now   lunatics wave good-bye
accepting despair by another name

Welcome new world to the brave old words
Peace   Hope   Justice
Truth Everlasting   welcome
ash-colored playground of children
happy in airy bags
never to touch is never to miss it

Scarface hello   we've got you covered
welcome untouchable   outlaw
with an alias in every country
salvos and roses   you are home
our footprints stamp you mortal

ELIZABETH ALEXANDER

APOLLO

We pull off
to a road shack
in Massachusetts
to watch men walk

on the moon. We did
the same thing
for three two one
blast off, and now

we watch the same men
bounce in and out
of craters. I want
a Coke and a hamburger.

Because the men
are walking on the moon
which is now irrefutably
not green, not cheese,

not a shiny dime floating
in a cold blue,
the way I'd thought,
the road shack people don't

notice we are a black
family not from there,
the way it mostly goes.
This talking through

static, bounces in space-
boots, tethered
to cords is much
stranger, stranger

even than we are.

RAYMOND ROSELIEP

EVA PSALM

i

The old white beard of God is blowing
on the moon,
Old Glory shivers on a winter clothesline,
a spider eagle dozes in the dust.
Two dancers dance:

Tender ghosts of twinned Nureyev,
tipsy on the straight-up legbeat
puffing halos out of cocoa grit,
gamboling colts in dreamtime motion,
Keystone cops a little fat,
kangaroos in water mirror
landing softshoe as the cat:
their feet keep falling free.

ii

Shadow heads Omega-point.
Light is flowing like a beard.

iii

I-Thou.
We're on the moon.
Aye, Thou.

Praise order, Jack-be-nimble,
praise *one small step*, Jack-man,
poke at the going embers of my life.
Hunt myself, Jack-hunter,
face up, Me-occupied.
Jubal, where's a harp, an organ?
Hang on a twig of language:
To that dance!

Ring.

Ring around those fat thieves
gathering up the moon,
run the keyboard of my ribs,
Jack! roll the wick still higher.
Shake the earth grain guilty
from each wrinkled sole,
jump your blood past limbo
of restricted birds.

Spring, dodge, spin,
wheel, loop, ride.
Fly inside.

The old white beard of God
is dancing on the moon.

In the first section, Nureyev refers to Rudolf Nureyev (1938–93), a Soviet ballet and contemporary dancer and choreographer, widely considered the greatest male ballet dancer of his generation. He defected from the USSR while in Paris in 1961. Jubal, in iv refers to Genesis 4:1, "the father of all who play stringed instruments and pipes."

PATRICIA SMITH

ANNIE PEARL SMITH DISCOVERS MOONLIGHT

My mother, the sage of Aliceville, Alabama,
didn't believe that men had landed on the moon.
"They can do anything with cameras,"
she hissed to anyone and everyone who'd listen,
even as moonrock crackled
beneath Neil Armstrong's puffed boot.
While the gritty film spun and rewound and we
heard the snarled static of "One small step,"
my mother pouted and sniffed
and slammed skillets into the sink.
She was not impressed.
After all, it was 1969, a year fat with deceit.
So many miracles
had proven mere staging for lesser dramas.

But why this elaborate prank
staged in a desert "somewhere out west,"
where she insisted the cosmic gag unfolded?
"They are trying to fool us."
No one argued, since she seemed near tears,

remembering the nervy deceptions of her own skin—
mirrors that swallowed too much,
men who blessed her with touch only as warning.
A woman reduced to juices, sensation and ritual,
my mother saw the stars only as signals for sleep.
She had already been promised the moon.

And heaven too. Somewhere above her head
she imagined bubble-cheeked cherubs
lining the one and only road to salvation,
angels with porcelain faces and celestial choirs
wailing gospel brown enough to warp the seams of paradise.
But for heaven to be real, it could not be kissed,
explored,
strolled upon
or crumbled in the hands of living men.
It could not be the 10 o'clock news,
the story above the fold,
the breathless garble of a radio "special report."

My mother had twisted her tired body into prayerful knots,
worked twenty years in a candy factory,
dipping wrinkled hands into vats of lumpy chocolate,
and counted out dollars with her thin, doubled vision,
so that a heavenly seat would be plumped for her coming.
Now the moon,
the promised land's brightest bauble,
crunched plainer than sidewalk beneath ordinary feet.
And her Lord just lettin' it happen.

"Ain't nobody mentioned God in all this," she muttered
over a hurried dinner of steamed collards and cornbread.
"That's how I know they ain't up there.
Them stars, them planets ain't ours to mess with.
The Lord woulda showed Hisself if them men
done punched a hole in my heaven."
Daddy kicked my foot beneath the table;

we nodded, we chewed, we swallowed.
Inside me, thrill unraveled;
I imagined my foot touching down on the jagged rock,
blessings moving like white light through my veins.

Annie Pearl Smith rose from sleep that night
and tilted her face full toward a violated paradise.
My father told me how she whispered in tongues,
how she ached for a sign
she wouldn't have to die to believe.

Now I watch her clicking like a clock toward deliverance,
and I tell her that heaven still glows wide and righteous
with a place waiting just for her,
fashioned long ago by that lumbering dance
of feet both human and holy.

CAMPBELL MCGRATH

APOLLO (1969)

This would be the vessel of our dismantling,
whose flames propose to outshine the divine
as science declares itself nemesis to myth.

What is science but a wondrous supposition
to shield yourselves from chaos, to explain,
as we once did, the order of the universe?

No, Helios's chariot does not transport the sun—
is that why you came, to steal his horses?
Is that why you voyaged to this negligible rock?

Earth, too, is a stone in a sea of darkness,
and now you are orphaned there, marooned
within your clouded atmosphere of reason.

Destroying us will not reduce your insignificance.
Selene, that beautiful dreamer, will not vanish
because you plant a banner on her orb.

Did you think the moon her residence? Fools.
She lives where all gods do, as everything
you exalt and rage against does: in you.

MOON LANDING

It's natural the Boys should whoop it up for
so huge a phallic triumph, an adventure
    it would not have occurred to women
    to think worth while, made possible only

because we like huddling in gangs and knowing
the exact time: yes, our sex may in fairness
    hurrah the deed, although the motives
    that primed it were somewhat less than *menschlich*.

A grand gesture. But what does it period?
What does it osse? We were always adroiter
    with objects than lives, and more facile
    at courage than kindness: from the moment

the first flint was flaked this landing was merely
a matter of time. But our selves, like Adam's,
    still don't fit us exactly, modern
    only in this—our lack of decorum.

Homer's heroes were certainly no braver
than our Trio, but more fortunate: Hector
      was excused the insult of having
      his valor covered by television.

Worth *going* to see? I can well believe it.
Worth *seeing*? Mneh! I once rode through a desert
      and was not charmed: give me a watered
      lively garden, remote from blatherers

about the New, the von Brauns and their ilk, where
on August mornings I can count the morning
      glories, where to die has a meaning,
      and no engine can shift my perspective.

Unsmudged, thank God, my Moon still queens the Heavens
as She ebbs and fulls, a Presence to glop at,
      Her Old Man, made of grit not protein,
      still visits my Austrian several

with His old detachment, and the old warnings
still have power to scare me: Hybris comes to
      an ugly finish, Irreverence
      is a greater oaf than Superstition.

Our apparatniks will continue making
the usual squalid mess called History:
      all we can pray for is that artists,
      chefs and saints may still appear to blithe it.

Originally published in the September 6, 1969, edition of the New Yorker—*just over a month after the moon landing had gripped the nation's collective imagination. Auden's dismissive account reads like a response to Archibald MacLeish's heroics-focused "Voyage to the Moon."*

ANNE SEXTON

MOON SONG, WOMAN SONG

I am alive at night.
I am dead in the morning,
an old vessel who used up her oil,
bleak and pale boned.
No miracle. No dazzle.
I'm out of repair
but you are tall in your battle dress
and I must arrange for your journey.
I was always a virgin,
old and pitted.
Before the world was, I was.

I have been oranging and fat,
carrot colored, gaped at,
allowing my cracked o's to drop on the sea
near Venice and Mombasa.
Over Maine I have rested.
I have fallen like a jet into the Pacific.
I have committed perjury over Japan.
I have dangled my pendulum,

my fat bag, my gold, gold
blinkedy light
over you all.

So if you must inquire, do so.
After all I am not artificial.
I looked long upon you,
love-bellied and empty,
flipping my endless display
for you, you my cold, cold
coverall man.

You need only request
and I will grant it.
It is virtually guaranteed
that you will walk into me like a barracks.
So come cruising, come cruising,
you of the blast off,
you of the bastion,
you of the scheme.
I will shut my fat eye down,
headquarters of an area,
house of a dream.

ALYSE BENSEL

LUNAR

Moons mothers blacked out. Our initials written beside
an emblem of absence. Perfect twenty-eight days apart

between the glossy pages of the wall calendar. What mattered
was the beginning, the forecast predictions set in oceanic

pelvic wanderings. Hysterical women were thought incurable
because their organs would not stay still. The uterus pulled

the body in accordance with the moon's orbit. As punishment
we spent blood-drained hours with the nurse before she ushered

us back to class. Our teachers shook their heads at the terror of girls
who wrapped hoodies around their hips, palmed tampons

as they shuffled toward the bathroom. The moon must have been
moving inside us. We gritted through the pain, learned to bear it,

nothing like labor, we were told. Our bodies boxed inside
the weeks, the months, the years. Now there are no longer

any moons: we are irregular from hormones or unpredictable
comets balling in the ovary or menopause, endometriosis.

Our pain with a shrug, a smile, a marked patience
for suffering as we wonder at the first men in padded

space suits who conquered a distant satellite
feared for centuries, their spaceship's trajectory

calculated by women. The men swept up in a new field
that released their bodies from heaviness. The women

anchored to the ground even as their hips split open
to new worlds that already existed. Every day meteorites

are hurled into the planet. The sound when the men re-entered
the atmosphere was impossible to predict—

no one could breathe from their diaphragms
to expel all that sharpness from their lungs.

GABRIELLE CALVOCORESSI

CAPTAIN LOVELL,

My eyes are shaky and glimmer like the stars.
My head turns to the left and it moves
just like a pendulum. The kids laugh and shake
it back to me, all the ways I'm stupid,
not like them. But I know how the grass sounds
when the locusts come, like a spaceship
taking off and how it makes the air shake.

Captain Lovell, I heard it in the branches
and the leaves. I heard the rocket leaving.
My teacher said it wasn't so, that you're
past hearing but my father said I could.
He puts his hands hard on my shoulders
from behind and holds my head still
with his looking. But I can feel how much

I want to shake and let myself go loose
and double like a cloud of mayflies on the lake,
you know just how they rise so you couldn't
see just one of them, not even with your thumb

held up to catch one with your eyes. It's something
I can't do that Babe and David can, can't sight
the stars or use a telescope or ever fire a gun.

Dr. Lovell, I like to think you're spinning
and can't feel it like I can't feel the world shake
unless I'm really tired and then it's like a gift
to let it go and just stop trying so hard. I like
to think you let go too and when the kids
run at me and move their heads from left
to right and call me "Zigzag" I look up

and wish myself up there with you
just calm and swinging through the stars.

AL WORDEN

INTO ORBIT

It's nerves:
The task is here now
Stay cool, they won't know,
And then it will be too late.
        I know I can do it.

A vibration, a roar,
Motion,
Shaking, rattling, we lift
        Straight up.

Lights flash, panel moves,
Floating in nothingness
Then softly,
        Softly, the motion begins again.

Push up the switch:
Suddenly, light everywhere
Slowly, softly, as in a dream
Streaking down
        Trying to return—too fast.

Flashes again, only more gentle,
Relief—everything works—
Is it possible?
Man is a fragile thing.
      Didn't we realize that?

Faster, faster, but
Only in numbers,
There is no speed,
No motion.
      Where are we?

This is a mistake:
Am I the only one who cares?
Upside-down
Trying to fall
Off
      the edge of the earth.

We've got to go on
Compelled by God knows what
To find answers
And rocks

And then—nothing;
Lights stop, hearts start,
In one monstrous moment
      We are in orbit.

BRUCE BOND

ELEGY FOR THE LAST MAN TO WALK THE MOON

I no longer have the luxury of being ordinary.
—GENE CERNAN

I too am restless. I say this and I do not
know you. My moon was never your moon,

as yours was never yours long but lost
among the rigs and waters of the gulf,

the wax and oiled shine of the harbor
a souvenir. I too was there. My face

in the otherwise darkened room lit
by TV feed. If I did not understand

your words of peace and hope, how you walked
with them and so gave voice to a thrall

of nerves unburdened in the dead still air,
I knew you as the more courageous version

of a boy, the one who would remain.
I want to ask that boy. Is paradise still

the thing on fire, first with joy, then joy
abandoned; does it scorch the eye of one

who comes, leaves, and, transported, breaks in two.
If I did not understand the reverie

of a man who walked the dark and looked back
at the watered iris of his planet,

haloed in a breathable dust, in paths
and perturbations of the spheres; I believed.

The blue marble was a mirror, the kind that breaks
the quotidian spectrum into one part

rock the other the scourge that makes it shine.
Call it hope, this place, this pure white salt,

just you (the flyboy) and your co-astronaut
(a specialist in rocks). Call it a minute,

an hour—whatever it was—you sat in cold
and vital silence, the landing gear extended.

Peace is always a little unearthly. You know this.
You know a host of words whose target slips

the cross of scopes and so becomes the flume
of myths and numbers chalked against darkness.

The hardest step is the first step home.
So you said, never again to leave the shadow-

stenciled footprint that survives a lifetime
undisturbed. The daughter's initial you sketched

with a finger in the silt, there, on your way
to the ladder, it was something you hoped

a future traveler would kneel to read,
the I-was-here that means nothing there,

as moon-dust does, but here below is priceless.
It was something you read over and over

before the outstretched microphones and flash
of newsmen in the faceless dark, something

years later in programmatic pleas to congress,
or later to the faithful at the local mall.

Something in the sharp and fatal beauty
of light that turned to near erasure when sun

was highest. Something that a child saw.
She sees it still. The child in the eye

among pedestrians at moonrise, south
of those refineries that litter the shore.

She thinks how enormous a moon becomes
at first, dredged upward from extinction.

I do not know her, but I say this, as one
says the word *joy* in the night that follows

and the long walk home. She looks back. Somewhere
a father's chronic distractions at the table,

the restless hand that tapped its coffee cup,
the man who held it, empty, in the air.

She knows and yet. Can never know. The eye
that crystals in the dark. Cold and vital.

RAY BRADBURY

ABANDON IN PLACE

*Three elegies written on visiting
the deserted rocket pads at Cape Canaveral*

1

Abandon in Place.
No Further Maintenance Authorized.
Abandon. Turn away your face.
No more the mad high wanderings of thought
You once surmised. Let be!
Wipe out the stars. Put out the skies.
What lived as center to our souls
Now dies—so *what?*—now dies.
What once as arrow to our thoughts
Which target-ran in blood-fast flow
No longer flies.
Cut off the stars. Slam shut the teeming skies.
Abandon in Place.
Burn out your eyes.

2

Where firebirds once
Now daubers caulk the seams;
Where firewings flew

To blueprint young men's dreams,
Now warbler here and osprey weave their nests
From laces lost from off a spaceman's tread.
The great hearthplace stands cold,
Its Phoenix dead.
No more from out the coals
Bright salamanders burn and gyre,
Only the bright beasts' skins and restless bones bed here,
And lost the fire.
O, Phoenix, rub thy bones,
No more suspire!
Flint souls, strike mind against wild mind.
Return! Be born of spent desire.
Bright burn. Bright burn!
O mighty God's voice, shorn,
Give shout next Easter morn. Be born!
(Our prayer calls you to life.)
Reborn of fire!

3

Abandon in Place.
So the sign says, so the words go.
The show is spent, the fire-walkers gone,
And gone the glow at dawn.
This day? No rockets rise like thunder.
The wonder still remains
In meadows where mound-dwellers not so long ago
Envied the birds, the untouched stars,
And let their touching envy grow.
Machineries stir here with falls of rust;
The lust for space still echoes
In the birds that circle lost in mourning cries
Repeating shouts of crowds long-spent
Whose aching shook the skies.
The sea moves down the shore
In wave on wave full-whispering,
No more. No more.

When will the harvesters return
To gather further wonders as a fuel
And let them burn?
How soon will all of Earth mob round, come here once more
To stop the night,
Put doubt away for good with rocket light?
O soon, O let that day be soon
When midnight blossoms with grand ships
As bright and high as noon.
Prepare the meadows, birds, and mounds,
Old ghosts of rocketmen, arise.
Fling up your ships, your souls, your flesh, your blood,
Your blinding dreams
To fill, refill, and fill again
Tomorrow and tomorrow and tomorrow's
Promised and re-promised
Skies.

ROBOTIC
EXPLORERS

N THE mid-twentieth century, public hopes of finding life on Mars remained high. Astronomer Percival Lowell's speculation about declining civilizations with massive canals had few scientific supporters, but popular science depictions of the Martian surface through the 1950s included simple plant and animal lifeforms. On July 15, 1965, Mariner 4 took the first close-up photographs of the surface of Mars during a flyby mission and shattered those hopes: the returning photographs revealed the Red Planet as deeply cratered and devoid of advanced lifeforms, with only a thin atmosphere surrounding it.

During the same era, our knowledge of the outer planets was limited to observations made by telescopes on the ground. We knew of a handful of moons and had seen the massive rings surrounding Saturn. In 1973, Pioneer 10 and 11 became the first human-made objects to pass through the asteroid belt, opening the way for the "Grand Tour" of the outer planets undertaken by Voyager 1 and 2 between 1979 and 1989. At Jupiter, Voyager 1 captured the first evidence of active volcanic activity beyond the surface of Earth—on the moon Io—as well as the first proof of lightning on another planet, in the gas giant's atmosphere. Voyager 2 offered the first ever close-up views of Uranus and Neptune, blue ice giants with dark rings accompanied by strange moons like Neptune's Triton, where geysers spew nitrogen ice.

Even into the twenty-first century, tiny Pluto was expected to be a geologically dead world, an inactive chunk of rock at the outer edge of the solar system. Even the Hubble Space Telescope can only make out regions of light and dark on Pluto's surface because of its small size and great distance from Earth. When the New Horizons spacecraft completed the first successful flyby in 2015, Pluto was unveiled as what principle investigator Alan Stern calls "a sci-fi planet," with red silica snow, mountains of water-ice as tall as the Rockies, and a blue atmosphere, Earth-like in color if not in composition.

It would be difficult to overstate how profoundly robotic exploration has altered our understanding of our solar system. Earth-based telescopes have offered glimpses of other planets for four centuries, since Galileo discovered Jupiter's four largest moons in 1610. But with the advent of robotic spacecraft, and the missions that sent them on journeys no human could undertake with modern technology, our knowledge of the solar system—our neighborhood in the vastness of space—has expanded exponentially, opening human imaginations to the stranger-than-fiction realities of our nearest neighbors in the cosmos. Over the past sixty years, robotic flyby spacecraft, orbiters, atmospheric probes, landers, and rovers have sent back massive amounts of scientific data to Earth, redefining our understanding of planets' atmospheres, magnetic fields, geologic features, rings, and moons. Importantly, these missions have also sent back photographs that have allowed us to experience this exploration as if with our own eyes.

The farthest humans have traveled from Earth's surface is 248,655 miles, the distance reached by the beleaguered crew of Apollo 13 as they passed the far side of the Moon in 1970 before returning to Earth. By contrast, as of 2020, Voyager 1 has traveled 13 billion miles away from Earth. Every second it treks farther from the sun, out beyond the ragged edge of our solar system, heading deep into interstellar space. The spacecraft itself will never return, but the data it collects continue to reach us here on Earth, allowing us by proxy to make the journey along with it.

Robotic spacecraft blur the boundaries of what exploration means. In writing about the twin Voyager spacecraft, constructed in the mid-1970s, historian Stephen J. Pyne describes the sources of that blurring:

> They were something more than dumb machines, because they had a degree of autonomy and had to act, within limits, independently of their handlers. They were more than a simple ganglia of instruments, because they carried their own motive power, which granted them the means to journey. Like any artifact of human contrivance, they exhibited a style that embodied the imagination and the values of their creators, which granted them a simulacrum of personality.

The poems in this section wrestle with that boundary between human and machine, vehicle and explorer, and how the new knowledge these robotic explorers send back changes the humans who receive it—both their understanding of the universe and of themselves.

Human concepts of connection, beauty, and meaning become fluid in the context of robotic missions. Donna Kane imagines Pioneer 10 leaving behind human ideas of loneliness to become "simply alone" as it travels beyond the asteroid belt, a tangible expression of human thought reaching across the solar system in search of an object. Dan Beachy-Quick and Srikanth Reddy consider photographs of Mars sent back by Opportunity, the plucky rover active from 2004 to 2018: an image "the machine captured by accident" in the course of acting within predefined limits reaches a computer screen on Earth and becomes "an aesthetic sensation" causing "a human nerve / To say: It's beautiful." Rejecting the idea that images from space can affirm the meaning of human emotions like love, Landis Everson chooses to delight instead in the "rich nitrogen and hydrocarbons, the bright / storm of the swirls and eddies" that turn up "near Phoebe's lifeless / dark material," images captured by Cassini during its flyby of Saturn's moon Phoebe in 2004.

Whether they offer confirmation of meaning, robotic missions extend into the distances of space because a human hand directs them to go, laden with desire. Few missions carry as much of our longing as the Voyager spacecraft. Poems engaging with the Voyager mission recur throughout this section, reflecting both the startling length of Voyager's continuing mission (more than four decades) and the profound appeal it has for nonscientists. Jessica Rae Bergamino gives voice to Voyager 1 as it takes the iconic "Family Portrait" of the solar system, a mosaic image of Earth, Venus, and the four outer planets taken more than four billion miles from Earth in 1990. Carl Sagan urged NASA to take the photograph, and it revealed Earth as what Sagan termed a "pale blue dot" among the planets, a speck amid immensity meant to help us understand our smallness. For Bergamino, the image displays Earth's longing mirrored back to itself, the spacecraft sent to explore boundless distances but ultimately turning toward Earth with a "last long gaze . . . her blue face becoming its own reflection."

Voyager's Golden Record—a twelve-inch phonograph record affixed to both spacecraft, carrying a message to any intelligent alien life that might encounter them as they continue their journey into interstellar space—has long captured the imagination of the public, rivalling the momentous scientific discoveries of the mission. Tomás Q. Morín describes the record as a "gilded handshake / to the stars" that, because of its lofty aspirations, fails to capture the more common condition of human apathy or the "clammy light" of "love / gone cold." Anthony Michael Morena's *The Voyager Record*, a series of prose poems, confronts the reality that the Record's message might be unintelligible for any alien life that would find it—and that in a sense it also becomes unintelligible for human listeners, whose cyclical life patterns differ from Voyager's journey into infinity. Srikanth Reddy's *Voyager*, a book-length sequence created by selectively erasing former U.N. Secretary-General Kurt Waldheim's memoir, confronts the human history of wartime atrocities carried over into spaceflight. In 1986, Waldheim's role as an intelligence officer for Nazi Germany and his knowledge of the murder of civilians came to light—almost a decade after his voice had been launched into space on behalf of humankind aboard the Golden Record. Heather Christle, writing about Voyager 1's passage beyond the boundary of our solar system in 2012, situates that event within "the year of evidence of chemical warfare" in Syria, "clear or uncertain // depending on where you live." Even nonhuman explorers are not exempt from the human evils of their time.

Burdened as they are with human failings, robotic spacecraft encapsulate the human desire to see, to know, and to understand. They extend our scientific knowledge and gesture toward our desire for the beautiful, the strange, and the unearthly. They speak to our longing to find in those most unearthly of places something familiar—life. Current and upcoming robotic missions prove the continuing power of this motivation. The possibility of human habitation on Mars will be explored in part by the Mars 2020 rover, while the Europa Clipper, set to launch in the 2020s, will return new data about the probable subsurface ocean on Jupiter's moon Europa, and whether that ocean might harbor life of any kind. OSIRIS-REx and Hayabusa2, both currently underway, seek to return samples of asteroids to Earth in the hopes of uncovering possible connections between asteroids and the formation of Earth's oceans. These robotic missions carry human vision far across the solar system and even deep into the time of its formation. Through poems, we can dwell in the wild possibilities that open there.

Julie Swarstad Johnson

DONNA KANE

PIONEER 10

Its shadow's been gone since lift-off

but it took light disappearing before lonely

seemed simply alone, or if not alone then deep

in the lab of the not understood, the not taste-of-ourselves

in its gold dust, the not soot-plumped sweat

of our brows incandescent with plutonium.

Shed of silver, quick, small—ideas burning off

like surplus fuel, the Pioneer 10 is a thought clicked

shut. Limbs drawn in, it drops like a tick

from the brain's limbic core, like a photon

traveling who knows for how long

before reaching a body,

the way the mind needs an object,

something to crack open on, and by its reflection, shine.

BRIAN TURNER

VIKING 1

*Viking Lander 1 made its final transmission to Earth
November 11, 1982*

On approach to Mars, dune fields in the distance,
the spacecraft descends within a storm of dust
before landing on the Golden Plain, Chryse Planitia,
which is a vast and stony desert, a graveyard
of shadows cast sanguine in their repose.

Cameras click in shuttered housings. The landscape
a pornographic scene caught in apertures
opened wide: sand tables in their martial aspect,
compass points, barchan dunes, the far horizon's body line
in rocky silhouette, where Earth is a small, warm light
rising zenith blue beyond the dusk, where I am still a boy,
barefoot on the wet grass of the San Joaquin valley,
the millions of miles between made closer by opposition.

In the old days, they say the desert Arabs hung lanterns
high in the date palms, a guide for friends and strangers
traveling by night. And maybe that's what I'm doing
as I search for lamps in the night's vast amphitheater,
even if I don't know how to put it into words—

I'm searching for the face on Mars, so much like our own,
made from dust and to dust returning, the wind's erosion
calling into the void with that brutal instrument, pain.
And like so many before me, I listen.
I want to hear how the great questions posed by ruin
are given the elegant response of stone.

How we, like Aphrodite, are seduced.

TOMÁS Q. MORÍN

GOLD RECORD

Dark was the night the *Voyager* slipped
into space carrying the music of one whale
greeting another, as well as the thud
of the stubborn heart and three,
maybe four, people laughing, the sum
of whose voices isn't that much different
from the few seconds of herded sheep,
at least to my poor, imperfect ear
that still has trouble distinguishing
a caterwaul from a stabbing victim,
two sounds our wise Sagan
did not include on his gilded handshake
to the stars, which is regrettable
because what better way to capture
our tempers and apathy than record
some pitiful soul, hand at his punctured
side, trying to groan louder than the TVs
the neighborhood keeps turning up
because they think he's a pair of cats
fucking under the luminous stars,

the very stars the *Voyager* will photograph
on the sly until it stumbles upon a ship
piloted by a race of beings so starved
for connection they cancel their plans
for the evening and sit on shag rugs—
their favorite souvenir from the seventies
—and cue our golden record
on the turntable they inherited
from their in-laws and never expected to use
for anything other than drinks and magazines
to entertain the occasional visitor, much less to hear
Blind Willie Johnson, that priest of the night
Sagan placed alongside Stravinsky
and company because in the three minutes
and twenty-one seconds Johnson sang for Columbia
in 1927 he moaned to the heavens
about homelessness or immortality or some
other mumbo jumbo any race smart enough to escape
gravity and cross the peacock-black
of galaxies would never believe because they
would know the blues are always about love
gone cold, and its light, the clammy light we might spend
years saying we can't live without and then do.

JOHN UPDIKE

AN OPEN LETTER TO VOYAGER II

Dear Voyager:
              This is to thank you for
The last twelve years, and wishing you, what's more,
Well in your new career in vacant space.
When you next brush a star, the human race
Will be a layer of old sediment,
A wrinkle of the primates, a misspent
Youth of some zoömorphs. But you, your frail
Insectoid form, will skim the sparkling vale
Of the void practically forever. As
The frictionless light-years and -epochs pass,
The rigid constellations Earth admires
Will shift and rearrange their twinkling fires.
No tipped antenna-dish will strain to hear
Your whispered news, nor poet call you dear.

Ere then, let me assure you you've been grand.
A little shaky at the outset, and
Arthritic in the swivel-joints, antique
In circuitry, virtually deaf, and weak

As a refrigerator bulb, you kept
Those picture postcards coming. Signals crept
To Pasadena; there they were enhanced
Until those planets clear as daylight danced.
The stripes and swirls of Jupiter's slow boil,
Its crazy moons—one cracked, one fried in oil,
One glazed with ice, and one too raw to eat,
Still bubbling with the juice of inner heat—
Arrived on our astonished monitors.
Then, following a station break of years,
Fat Saturn rode your feeble beam, and lo!—
Not corny as we feared, but Art Deco—
The hard-edge, Technicolor rings; they spin
At different speeds, are merely meters thin,
And cast a flash-bulb's shadows. Planet three
Was Uranus (accented solemnly,
By anchormen, on the first syllable,
Lest viewers think the "your" too personal):
A glassy globe of gas upon its side,
Its nine faint braided rings at last descried,
Its corkscrew-shaped magnetic passions bared,
Its pocked attendants digitized and aired.
Last loomed, against the Oort Cloud, blue Neptune,
Its counterrevolutionary moon,
Its wispy arcs of rings and whitish streaks
Of unpredicted tempests—thermal freaks,
As if an unused backyard swimming pool,
Remote from stirring sunlight, dark and cool
(Sub-sub-sub-freezing), chose to make a splash.
Displays of splendid waste, of rounded trash!
Your looping miles of guided drift brought home
How fruitless cosmic space would be to roam.
One awful ball succeeds another, none
Fit for a shred or breath of life. Our lone
Delightful, verdant orb was primed to cede
The H_2O and O and N we need.
Your survey, in its scrupulous depiction,

Purged from the solar system science fiction—
No more Uranians or Io-ites,
Just Earthlings dreaming through their dewy nights.

You saw where we could not, and dared to go
Where we would be destroyed; you showed
A kind of metal courage, and faithfulness.
Your cryptic, ciphered, graven messages
Are for ourselves, designed to boomerang
Back like a prayer from where the angels sang,
That shining ancient blank encirclement.
Your voyage now outsoars mundane intent
And joins blind matter's motion. *Au revoir*,
You rickety free-falling man-made star!
Machines, like songs, belong to all. A man
Aloft is Russian or American,
But you aloft were simply sent by Man
At large.
                Sincerely yours,
                        A fan.

JESSICA RAE BERGAMINO

AFTER TAKING THE FAMILY PORTRAIT OF THE SOLAR SYSTEM, VOYAGER ONE UNDERSTANDS HERSELF AS ORPHEUS IN PLAIN DAYLIGHT

Valentine's Day, 1990

Past Pluto, I turned to watch the pale thrill
of Earth spinning on without me.

We both knew I could never return—
she was already warring cold, beginning,

even then, to melt. But what's true about leaving
is true about looking back—both require doubt

for poignancy. & if I'm honest, we all know I turned
because she called. I'd always been a mirror for her will.

So this is how I measure distance: not in the leaving,
but in the being left. In the absence of touch. The billions.

In small orbits strung upon small orbits, spinning
to some celestine harmony we never were meant to count.

I sent all I could across the distance—thrills of zeros
and ones dimming to data on an astronomer's desk.

How she saw herself, then—fragrant, green,
lit by the smear of sun, a bright crescent hung

beside Venus' flame, both of them pocked
by longing. She thought she was center of the universe

once, and how close she was, straddled by fortune
while Neptune and Uranus clung to the dark edges

of sight. So, yes, I turned, because who doesn't deserve
to see ourselves in the ghost of what loves us?

& she sang in code to celebrate, programming my eyes
to close and never open, making sure my last long gaze

was her blue face becoming its own reflection.
How silly I was to call this a love letter.

Somewhere, Mercury is retrograde.

SRIKANTH REDDY

FROM *VOYAGER*

Book Two

In November last year, I became interested in the
fate of a machine which had been launched into
creation and disappeared from sight during my
boyhood. The thought of it roaming our system
unconcerned about the policies of the regime
was a relief from the strains and suspicions that
surrounded us at home. Every morning, I would
visit the library to dig out information for my
dissertation on the principles of writing, and in
the night, overhead, sought refuge in the parallel
journey.

Aboard, I read, was a deeply-etched record of the world that floated away, full of popular tunes and beautiful technological problems. Perhaps an observer far in outer space might study this information in days to come. He would have to weigh carefully in his heart the words of a man who by some quirk of fate had become a spokesman for humanity, who could give voice to all the nations and peoples of the world, and, so to speak, the conscience of mankind.

This man, legend states, likely knew of the mass execution of groups of people as a capable officer required to collect and analyze data, prepare reports, conduct investigations, and otherwise facilitate operational projects in the last world war. At the time, however, he did not express concern at this action. To a degree this is understandable. His voice failed. Now, after years have passed, our little record is carrying his words as Secretary General of the United Nations to a government above.

ANTHONY MICHAEL MORENA

FROM *THE VOYAGER RECORD:* *A TRANSMISSION*

I like the indifferent greetings the most, the hesitant ones. The Rajasthani greeting says: "We are happy here and you be happy there." The Arabic greeting is less indifferent, but still wary. It says: "Greetings to our friends in the stars. May time bring us together." Which doesn't tell the aliens not to come, but maybe not to come over just yet.

We cast this message into the cosmos. It is likely to survive a billion years into our future, when our civilization is profoundly altered and the surface of the Earth may be vastly changed.

Carter tells them straight up: listen, aliens, idk but the planet won't necessarily be the same place that it is now lol don't expect any warm welcomes. Don't expect me. It was prescient. Carter watched the Aral Sea go from Soviet-planned irrigation project to desert wasteland where ghost ships rust in the sun. He disappeared whole prairies underneath affordable houses.

You better believe we'll be "profoundly altered," aliens.

The aliens who discover the Voyager record are confused by the 55 greetings. They have difficulty with linguistics. Is each word a separate meaning? What does one word have to do with the next? Does each word represent the sounds of a different language? Does each phoneme? Where does one word end and the next word begin? Is this one language with many facets to it, expressing with sound a mood, a face to each feeling, a so-many chambered heart—like the aliens' heart, which has fourteen? Why, 55 times, do these people say the same thing over and over? Did they think that we would not get the point?

The essential difference between a robotic mission like Voyager and a crewed mission is the difference between a linear narrative and a cyclical one. We want people to come back to the circling world, like a record, so we can start again. From scratch. A cycle's humanity is its finality: it has to end somewhere, it has to begin again. Voyager, on the other hand, may never stop.

As I listen to the Bulgarian folk song "Izlel je Delyo Hagdutin," I picture your destruction by a thousand micro-impacts spread out over time in the empty regions of space, in the Oort cloud, which I imagine as dust, or space filled with dust, hard rock bits, and ice. Battered, the Voyager craft rolls away from each hit, as you play this song as accompanying soundtrack. The transmission dish shatters without noise; Voyager lists and is cold. This was not a suicide mission, but no extra steps were made to protect you other than to put a cover on you. They did not bury you in a black box deep within the craft. Does it make you a more valid artistic work that you were never viable? If you are ever found, what will be left will not be you but something unintentional. Each impact makes another tiny perforation in you, punctuating song. You become a remix: not many songs, but one. "Izlel je Delyo Hagdutin" is about a legendary Bulgarian bandit-rebel who took to the hills to fight the imperial rule of the Ottoman Turks, who were massacring whole villages. People said he couldn't be killed by ordinary means, but only by a silver bullet. That is how they got him. You are made of gold plated-copper, so I never had as much hope for you. It's a shepherdess' song, with bagpipes in it, playing just like this was a cop's funeral.

LANDIS EVERSON

CASSINI IN HEAVEN

The robotic Global Martian Surveyor
seeing a dozen circular craters
landed in a depression, in dust, forgot

stored orders. A cold beauty looking for ghosts
within range, looking for another us on a planet raw,
a really different kind of orbit to operate through

layers, which are wrapped in a "harmonious symphony."
"Queen Mary will host a major space conference," her crown
realized in "sunlight from the upper left." A thin

wind, but no windmills. No moon named Triste. This
is the way onions act, peeling layers and wobbling.
Cassini saw a halo of moons, Saturn's metaphorically-

layered rings, not unlike a pearl necklace whirling
heartlessly, tearlessly, cut into rock, drilling
down to the ring-spinning pearl beauty. "Pearl onions,"

and I laughed, rich nitrogen and hydrocarbons, the bright
storm of the swirls and eddies near Phoebe's lifeless
dark material. Wouldn't it be another laugh if the

metaphor exploded our whole Theory of Innocence?
The mechanical tears gravitate into real moons.
"There's something I have to tell you," one of the

astronauts whispered, forgetting we were listening. The President
a vast void beyond our concept of good and evil, the
sun a hot dot, dead dustballs. So, not everything reflects love.

---

*Everson's "Global Martian Surveyor" may refer to the Mars Global Surveyor, a NASA
orbiter that mapped Mars between 1996 and 2007. He could also simply be referring to
one of the many failed Mars landers: nearly 60 percent of all international missions to
Mars have failed prematurely.*

DAN BEACHY-QUICK AND SRIKANTH REDDY

FROM *CONVERSITIES*

I I

The lander turns its lens to photograph its tracks
Stretching across the red dust back to horizon,
Conducts a test to see what this world lacks,

Corrects its own path, witness the confusion
In the red dirt where the boulder's shadow
Leans across the path, an aesthetic sensation

The machine captured by accident whose glow
On the computer screen excites a human nerve
To say: It's beautiful. A world absent sorrow.

One must have a mind of winter / to observe . . .
No, scratch that. *One must have a mind
Of winter / to regard* . . . The infinitesimal curve

Of horizon, extended off-screen, will round
Itself into unending. Figure eleven. The word
Beyond stamped on a speckled egg I found

In *Art News* last winter, the remains of a bird
Unborn forever within. Shake it, and it rattles—
A child's toy. Oology, we admit, is an absurd

Hobby, nonetheless popular—a crossword riddle
Answer in the Sunday Times—from a century
In which we live no longer, when the cattle-

Bird's egg displayed on the mantle, penury
Now, but then a wealth, as through a telescope,
Quaint hobby, Venus, Mars, Jupiter, and watery

Saturn are each an egg in orbit's nest . . . Tired tropes . . .
I tire of them, and you tire of them, whoever you are.
My mind is *a nothing that is* hanging from a rope.

---

*The italicized phrases quote Wallace Stevens's poem "The Snow Man," originally pub-
lished in 1923 in Stevens's first collection,* Harmonium *(Knopf).*

MARK A. MCCUTCHEON

VOYAGER 2, THINKING, TYPES THINGS

Very very very very very small
Billion miles recalculating
We don't know details well at all
The direction we were last going

Calculable but undetectable
Earth would be the one-yard line
As bright planets are invisible
Now does not exist in space-time

Outer solar system missions
With the winds from other stars
As in trigintillion years never

But please do send invitations
People might think there are bears
To hear from you by tomorrow over

Author's note: This sonnet-cento (a cento is a poem constructed entirely of lines from other poems) is composed of lines excerpted from tweets by @NSFVoyager2, the unofficial Twitter account of the Voyager 2 spacecraft. The title remixes that of the song "Thinking Voyager 2 Type Things" by Bob Geldof from the album The Vegetarians of Love *(Atlantic, 1990).*

CAROLYN OLIVER

ENCELADUS CONSIDERS *CASSINI*

Little witness, golden angler fish, plunge
and surface: you'll never take my measure.

Trawl for signs of life, hurl my reflection
home, swim through vapor curtains draining

me to chalk this boundary ornament,
this filmy ring I can't escape—I know

your exquisite instruments cannot scrape
my craters smooth, or catch my ocean's heave

and seething hiss. Nor can your innards taste
the ice that's never seen my father's face.

Old Saturn, child-eater. I've watched you jump
through his hoops, well trained. His patient maw waits

while your gods arc you close. Soon, mission's end:
a lick of flame snuffed out to keep me safe.

HEATHER CHRISTLE

HOW LONG IS THE HELIOPAUSE

They say before you know you want
to move your hand
                        your hand
is already about to move
They say in advance
                        these things
are decided

The box of cereal says *We're so happy
our paths have crossed*
                        but I do not think
I am on one
            I think I am in
a pathless field

The wind sends seeds abroad
                        The most careful engineering
Still these contrary gardens grow

They say it is hard to believe
that when robots are taking pictures

of Titan's orange ethane lakes
poets still insist on writing about their divorces

This is a poem for my husband
on the occasion of *Voyager*
                               perhaps having left our solar system
perhaps about to leave it very soon
                                 They cannot say
The message takes so long to drift to reach us

When the self-driving car wants to move
it will first say so
                changing lanes
                        changing lanes
                               changing lanes
It hesitates it does not know it is lost
or it has decided on always changing

I've heard the cat who may be alive
or may be dead should expect
to live forever
                progressively growing
sicker and sicker

This is for my husband
whom I expect to come home
some time between now and the future

Let me date this very clearly

This is the year after the year
when people with cable began
to pile Christmas lights into glass jars

the year of evidence of chemical warfare
clear or uncertain
                    depending on where you live

One beast lives one grows sicker and sicker
One dies one yowls at the door

Two days from now I will either
bleed or not bleed
                    I will remember
that four years ago we wed and asked
for Divine Assistance
                    though we neither of us
pray to any god

This is for him on the occasion
of the Olympian's indictment

They say he shot
the one he loved
                    Shot the one
who through a door
                    he could not see

None of this has been right
but maybe a tiny electrical god
has cut and spliced us together

And in this moment yes and in this moment no
and in this moment all the lights
go off at once and it is a bomb
or it is a daughter

And this great sound replaces the others
so I can hear nothing but the brightness
of the field
                   where I am waiting for the warm chest
of my husband
                        for its occasion
and if they say a word now
it would take years for me to know

JULIE SWARSTAD JOHNSON

PSALM 8

If you let it, the moon will tell you
your smallness: fragile creature on a tilted planet

facing the open darkness while the sun
burns on beyond your sight. We have so long now

denied that we think we are the center,
the Copernican sun firmly anchored in the sky

we swing through, but I write to you
as one who knows her own heart. So I say to you

blessed is the wild distance of the night,
the gauzy light of nebulas reaching us long after

they're gone. Blessed are the asteroids,
those fragments of the beginning which we did not

create, blessed the spacecraft that goes
to bring a piece back to us, the origin of oceans

maybe written in its dust. Blessed, too,
those machines that go without thought of return,

the glimpses they send back of worlds
we thought we knew: the opalescent whorls

of storms churning on Jupiter, liquid pooled deep
beneath the south pole of Mars, faintest sunlight

kindling Pluto's peaks of ice bright as sacred flame.
Blessed, all the universe beyond us and we

who hunger and thirst to know it, shadowed
on the earth, calculating the trajectories of light.

HUMANS IN LOW EARTH ORBIT

ON JANUARY 28, 1986, after the nation had been shocked by the destruction of the space shuttle Challenger seventy-three seconds into its flight, President Ronald Reagan's address on the disaster concluded with lines from a poem. The poem, John Gillespie Magee Jr.'s "High Flight," had sprung to mind for Reagan's speechwriter Peggy Noonan as she watched and rewatched the footage of Challenger's crew. "We will never forget them," Reagan read at his desk in the Oval Office, "nor the last time we saw them, this morning, as they prepared for their journey and waved goodbye and 'slipped the surly bonds of earth' to 'touch the face of God.'" For Noonan, Magee's poem "spoke of the joy of flying," a key drive that she paired with the desire to explore, regardless of the risks. "We've grown used to the idea of space," Noonan wrote earlier in the speech, "and perhaps we forget that we've only just begun. We're still pioneers."

Personal accounts by Reagan and Noonan indicate that they both experienced the Challenger address as a failure immediately after it was given, the speech too small a gesture or not eloquent enough to be meaningful given the scale of the tragedy. By the next morning, a flood of thanks and congratulatory notes proved their assessment incorrect: the public had experienced the address as deeply moving, comforting, and even visionary.

For some space policy experts, the space shuttle program is largely a failure. Following the captivating success of the Apollo moon landings, public and political interest in spaceflight quickly waned across the 1970s as the costly and morally devastating war in Vietnam raged on. Americans went to the Moon, but not to stay, and plans for missions to Mars or the establishment of space colonies withered. In that post-Apollo void, the space shuttle was presented to President Richard Nixon as a reliable, cost-effective approach that could meet scientific, military, and commercial needs, flying more than forty missions a year. But with the challenging dual goals of saving money and meeting demanding technical requirements related to military payloads, the shuttle as it finally launched in 1981 was a very different vehicle from what anyone had hoped for. Across its thirty years of operation and 135 missions on five completed orbiters—Columbia, Challenger, Discovery, Atlantis, and Endeavor—it would never live up to what had been promised of it.

Yet for the American public, the shuttle is one of the most recognizable images of the space program. Former NASA chief historian Roger Launius describes the space shuttle program as "an important symbol of the United States' technological capability, universally recognized as such by both the American people and the international community." The space shuttle era was ultimately one of impressive technical and scientific achievement; low Earth orbit—the limit of the shuttle orbiter's range—may not have been a new frontier, but the public often experienced it as if it were.

The length of the shuttle program's existence and the diversity of the crews who flew on the five orbiters made it a program that felt familiar, part of the fabric of public life that the poems in this section inhabit. Maxine Kumin places a shuttle launch within the context of "a city of people gathered on the beach" including "babies in Snuglis" and toddlers trailing "ancient blankets." Patrick McGuinness connects the space shuttle with childhood illness, a fever raging in his body transformed into the shuttle and "the story / of the fire that drove it on and up." In the poetry of Adrian Matejka, the shuttle program and specifically Guy Bluford, the first African American in space, becomes emblematic of new opportunity and Black achievement. In Matejka's "Those Minor Regrets," as in Mary Jo Salter's "A Kiss in Space," knowledge of human spaceflight is mediated by popular representations on television and other news media. Matejka's young speaker imagines spaceflight as "jetting through stars strobing," evoking the warp speed blurs of *Star Trek: The Next Generation*. Salter's speaker encounters space in the *New York Times*, clipping out a photograph of cosmonaut Yelena Kondakova kissing American astronaut Norm Thagard and wondering what the mundane Earth becomes for those who have traveled beyond it.

Although the space shuttle orbiters never left low Earth orbit, they facilitated views into the vast distances of space via telescopes operated beyond Earth's atmosphere, most famously the Hubble Space Telescope. Two-term U.S. Poet Laureate (2017–19) Tracy K. Smith records memories of her father, an engineer who worked on Hubble before its launch, in "My God, It's Full of Stars," another poem that links fact and fiction with numerous references to *2001: A Space Odyssey*, among other science-fiction movies. As the poem closes, Smith writes, "We saw to the edge of all there is." But that new sight brings no comfort or finality. Instead, the extreme distance of space and time glimpsed by Hubble is "so brutal and alive it seemed to comprehend us back." By contrast, Adrienne Rich in "Hubble Photographs: After Sappho," experiences the vastness of the universe seen by Hubble as a relief. Compared to the gaze of the beloved, Rich envisions the startling architectures of distant galaxies as "something // more desirable" because "they don't look back and we cannot hurt them." Rich, like Carl Sagan in his depiction of Earth as a "pale blue dot," finds perspective and comfort in the universe's largeness.

The space shuttle era provided a legacy of new vision and new possibility, but it is one scarred with loss. Tragedy most emphatically entered the story of American spaceflight with the deaths of the three crewmembers of Apollo 1, but reached its fullest expression with the televised destruction of Challenger at launch in 1986 and Columbia during reentry in 2003. In "Elegy for Challenger," Diane Ackerman, who had been a semifinalist for NASA's never-realized journalist-in-space project, elevates the shuttle to the realm of mythology, the Challenger crew "riding a golden plume," their mission "to pitch an outpost / in our wilderness of doubt." Betty Adcock's "Fallen," written after the destruction of Columbia, offers instead a clear-eyed refusal of such elevation: "Don't recoil," she writes early in the poem as she describes the buzzards who revealed the crash site. "Do / not imagine this a story to be tamed by naming / heroes who died for country." Spaceflight, which the shuttle program attempted to frame as routine, remained fraught with danger.

Less obvious dangers pervade time spent in low Earth orbit. Among these are long-term effects on the human body from extended time in space: loss of bone and muscle mass, exposure to radiation, headaches, nausea, and minor memory loss. Astronaut Story Musgrave, the only astronaut to fly aboard all five shuttle orbiters and who participated in space walks to repair the flawed optics of Hubble, describes seeing cosmic rays cause flashes in his vision in "Cosmic Fireflies." Keith Flynn considers "amnesia's simple fog" and the isolation in which astronauts on the ISS "do lonely things." Alison Hawthorne Deming invokes the year-long ISS sojourn of Scott Kelly beginning in 2015, and she reminds us that in the years of the space shuttle and space station, global warming and climate change became an unmistakable reality ever more widely experienced by the public. "Space might the be only way / to see the kind of sky we need," Deming writes, contending that, as we become more comfortable with a vantage point above the surface of Earth, we should be reminded of the biosphere's fragility.

The space shuttle program ended when the orbiter Atlantis touched down at the Kennedy Space Center on July 21, 2011, after a successful mission to the ISS. Over three decades, the program had become a fixture in the American mental landscape. The space shuttle program, like Apollo before it, left a void difficult to immediately fill. In the years following the shuttle's retirement, commercial ventures have emerged and demonstrated their reliability. Elon Musk's SpaceX now routinely delivers payloads into orbit, resupplies the ISS using the Dragon spacecraft, and even lands and reuses booster rockets. NASA's Commercial Crew Program has contracted with SpaceX and Boeing to launch humans into space from American soil, something that hasn't occurred since 2011.

Even with commercial enterprises underway, NASA, with the European Space Agency, continues to develop a spacecraft to return humans to the Moon and to take them beyond: Orion, an Apollo-style paired service module and conical command module designed for water landings, carrying a crew of four astronauts. When NASA conducted its first uncrewed test flight of Orion in December 2014, the spacecraft carried with it a plaque bearing Maya Angelou's 1995 poem "A Brave and Startling Truth." First read at the United Nations' fiftieth anniversary celebration, Angelou's poem invokes an expansive vision of human cooperation and achievement. Speaking in a ceremony at NASA headquarters following Orion's test flight, NASA administrator Charles Bolden spoke to the future of the space program and the unique ability of art to comment on it:

> It is fitting that Maya Angelou's prophetic words be flown not only outside the bounds of our Earth, but on the maiden voyage of a spacecraft that represents humanity's aspirations to move beyond our planet, to reach higher, and become more than we have ever been. Through art, and the unique perspective of people like Maya Angelou, our discoveries, and the new facts and expanded understanding brought to us by exploration, are transformed into meaning.

Scheduled for 2020, an Orion spacecraft will undertake the first mission of the Artemis program, which will put the uncrewed vessel in retrograde orbit of the Moon, 37,000 miles above the Moon's surface. A crewed version of the flight is slated for 2022. As of this writing, NASA hopes to create an international lunar-orbiting station called the Lunar Gateway and to return Americans, including the first woman, to the lunar surface in a sustainable fashion, starting in 2024. These stepping-stones back out into space all have human voyages to Mars firmly in view as the ultimate destination.

As we turn toward new milestones in spaceflight and look back on a history of more than sixty years, poetry allows us to question, dream, and struggle toward meaning. Howard Nemerov, reflecting on a launch of Atlantis during the space shuttle program's first decade, wrote, "What yet may come of this? We cannot know." We are witnessing a new age of reaching farther into space; through poetry, we linger in wonder on that threshold of unknowing.

Julie Swarstad Johnson

HOWARD NEMEROV

WITNESSING THE LAUNCH OF THE SHUTTLE ATLANTIS

So much of life in the world is waiting, that
This day was no exception, so we waited
All morning long and into the afternoon.
I spent some of the time remembering
Dante, who did the voyage in the mind
Alone, with no more nor heavier machinery
Than the ghost of a girl giving him guidance;

And wondered if much was lost to gain all this
New world of engine and energy, where dream
Translates into deed. But when the thing went up
It was indeed impressive, as if hell
Itself opened to send its emissary
In search of heaven or "the unpeopled world"
(thus Dante of doomed Ulysses) "behind the sun."

So much of life in the world is memory
That the moment of the happening itself—
So rich with noise and smoke and rising clear
To vanish at the limit of our vision

Into the light blue light of afternoon—
Appeared no more, against the void in aim,
Than the flare of a match in sunlight, quickly snuffed.

What yet may come of this? We cannot know.
Great things are promised, as the promised land
Promised to Moses that he would not see
But a distant sight of, though the children would.
The world is made of pictures of the world,
And the pictures change the world into another world
We cannot know, as we knew not this one.

MAXINE KUMIN

NIGHT LAUNCH

Canaveral Seashore National Park

Full moon. Everyone in silhouette
graying just this side of color as we wait:
babies in Snuglis, toddlers from whose clutches
ancient blankets depend, adults encumbered
with necklaces of cameras, binoculars.
A city of people gathered on the beach.
Expectant boats jockeying offshore.

When we were kids we used to race
reciting *the seething sea ceaseth;*
thus the sea sufficeth us
and then collapse with laughter, never
having seen the rise-and-fall of ocean,
the lip of foam like seven-minute icing,
moon-pricked dots of plankton skittering.

The horizon opens, floods with daybreak,
a rosy sunrise as out of sync
as those you fly into crossing the Atlantic,
midnight behind you, the bald sky blank,

and up comes the shuttle, one costly Roman candle,
orange, silent, trailing as its rockets fall
away, a complicated snake of vapor.

Along the beach a feeble cheer.
Muffled thumps of blastoff, long after,
roll like funeral drums, precise and grave.
We are the last to leave.
Driving back along the asphalt, signed
every hundred yards Evacuation Route
past honeycombs of concrete condominiums
I remember how we wrapped and carried
our children out to a suburban backyard
to see Sputnik cross the North Temperate Zone
at two in the morning, and how we shivered
watching that unwinking little light
move east without apparent cause.
On this warm seacoast tonight
in the false dawn my neckhairs rose.
Danger flew up to uncertain small applause.

ADRIAN MATEJKA

THOSE MINOR REGRETS

after Lynda Hull

We ran around Carriage House East
nonstop like a bunch of nervous mouths—

in jacking-jawing & split orbits—

& the huffing in the throat stack

& double-ply knee cracks as we slid
       Toughskin thick past the dented

    chariots on blocks & lover-graffitied
dumpsters, one after another in industrious,

planetary circuitry. All this disco symmetry,

    this sectioned happenstance
jangling our poked-out vertebrae

& vacant middles & the halogen lights
       shone clearly against

the chocolate bar as I slipped it
into my pocket at the Village Pantry.

Garrett said, *Man, just take it*, & I did.
        My first disobedient
accident after my father split.

        My first calculable maleficence,
guilt now sitting in my center
        like the powdered milk

        everybody drinks sometimes.

Back when I still wanted
        to be an astronaut—
        in a space shuttle

jetting through stars strobing
        as brightly as the front-row
kids we clowned habitually.

        Right before my nearsightedness
made blurs out of the teacher's
        chalk work, extension cords

        & raised hands out
        of branches & leaves.

        Right above my stomach's

tricky punch, right next to the busted
        harmony of heartbeats

where I sewed a yard-sale
        Star Trek patch thinking

Cynthia might like it.

Even the front-row kids
made fun of me for that.

How could I know?
Poor only matters around
        people who aren't poor

& everyone I knew was already
        a trivial thief. Even after

our electric cut off, some needier

neighbor tried to break into
our dark looking for some thing—

just like the sad, redheaded guy

        watching from the same
        Washington Square bench

across from the Flintstones ride
& 25¢ carousel of grinning bunnies

        & horses no one ever rode
        while we waited for the cops
to answer my mother's 911.

After every break-in, to the mall—

safety in the splendor of big cookies
        & pretzel salt, that spinning

disco ball out in Spencer's window

        the closest things to another
        world I can remember.

PATRICK MCGUINNESS

THE SHUTTLE

That swollen winter lying glandular
in my half-hallucinated rain-forest
of a bedroom, I watched myself drifting
to the window on a tide of perspiration.
Pyjamas like cling film, eyelids in flames,
I tuned in and out of the fever they thought
would *take me—where* I never knew,
nobody said, I was just the passenger
and this the tropical winter of my brush with
(low whispers) *what comes after,* something dim
I knew I touched but could not see.

Alone for hours I watched the shuttle graze
its night-acres, padding the black obsidian
fields of space to the echoes of long gone,
still-reverberating blasts; I heard white noise,
saw blackouts, ran my mind along the edge
of placeless voices calling *lift off and do you read . . .*

. . . for weeks, my fever

was the shadow of that shuttle, the story
of the fire that drove it on and up.
I dreamed I ran the cratered prairies
of the moon; in slow motion or at the speed
of light Christmas came and went,
people moved like wallpaper through the room.
Their shadows stayed long after they were gone.

　　　　　In my bloated head I screened
replay after replay of take-off, watched
as in mid-air the shuttle hung like a lobbed
newspaper frozen in its arc, cast half
its body aside in a blaze of fire; then,
rising, kicked it back, threw off its earthly self
and as I too rose it was like stripping off
my life in layers;

　　　　　　　I unlocked the ceiling,
head burning, face on fire, my twelve years
the debris that fell back, the chaos
I climbed free of as I walked on air,

and woke weeks later to find myself still here.

DIANE ACKERMAN

ELEGY FOR *CHALLENGER*

Wind-walkers,
how we envied you

riding a golden plume
on a glitter-mad trajectory

to watch Earth roll
her blooming hips below

and scout the shores
of still unnamed seas.

You were the Balboas
we longed to be,

all star-spangled grin,
upbeat and eager,

a nation's cameo.
When the sun went out

and you blew into your shadow,
horrors clanged

like falling bells.

You orbit our thoughts now
as last we saw you:

boarding a shuttle bound
out of this world,

quivering with thrill,
deadset, but tingling

to pitch an outpost
in our wilderness of doubt,

and climb that old ladder
whose rungs lead only higher.

We still dream your dream,
though we taste your fire.

TRACY K. SMITH

MY GOD, IT'S FULL OF STARS

1.

We like to think of it as parallel to what we know,
Only bigger. One man against the authorities.
Or one man against a city of zombies. One man

Who is not, in fact, a man, sent to understand
The caravan of men now chasing him like red ants
Let loose down the pants of America. Man on the run.

Man with a ship to catch, a payload to drop,
This message going out to all of space. . . . Though
Maybe it's more like life below the sea: silent,

Buoyant, bizarrely benign. Relics
Of an outmoded design. Some like to imagine
A cosmic mother watching through a spray of stars,

Mouthing *yes, yes* as we toddle toward the light,
Biting her lip if we teeter at some ledge. Longing
To sweep us to her breast, she hopes for the best

While the father storms through adjacent rooms
Ranting with the force of Kingdom Come,
Not caring anymore what might snap us in its jaw.

Sometimes, what I see is a library in a rural community.
All the tall shelves in the big open room. And the pencils
In a cup at Circulation, gnawed on by the entire population.

The books have lived here all along, belonging
For weeks at a time to one or another in the brief sequence
Of family names, speaking (at night mostly) to a face,

A pair of eyes. The most remarkable lies.

2.

Charlton Heston is waiting to be let in. He asked once politely.
A second time with force from the diaphragm. The third time,
He did it like Moses: arms raised high, face an apocryphal white.

Shirt crisp, suit trim, he stoops a little coming in,
Then grows tall. He scans the room. He stands until I gesture,
Then he sits. Birds commence their evening chatter. Someone fires

Charcoals out below. He'll take a whiskey if I have it. Water if I don't.
I ask him to start from the beginning, but he goes only halfway back.
That was the future once, he says. *Before the world went upside down.*

Hero, survivor, God's right hand man, I know he sees the blank
Surface of the moon where I see a language built from brick and bone.
He sits straight in his seat, takes a long, slow high-thespian breath,

Then lets it go. *For all I know, I was the last true man on this earth.* And:
May I smoke? The voices outside soften. Planes jet past heading off or back.
Someone cries that she does not want to go to bed. Footsteps overhead.

A fountain in the neighbor's yard babbles to itself, and the night air
Lifts the sound indoors. *It was another time*, he says, picking up again.

We were pioneers. Will you fight to stay alive here, riding the earth

Toward God-knows-where? I think of Atlantis buried under ice, gone
One day from sight, the shore from which it rose now glacial and stark.
Our eyes adjust to the dark.

3.

Perhaps the great error is believing we're alone,

That the others have come and gone—a momentary blip—

When all along, space might be choc-full of traffic,

Bursting at the seams with energy we neither feel

Nor see, flush against us, living, dying, deciding,

Setting solid feet down on planets everywhere,

Bowing to the great stars that command, pitching stones

At whatever are their moons. They live wondering

If they are the only ones, knowing only the wish to know,

And the great black distance they—we—flicker in.

Maybe the dead know, their eyes widening at last,

Seeing the high beams of a million galaxies flick on

At twilight. Hearing the engines flare, the horns

Not letting up, the frenzy of being. I want it to be

One notch below bedlam, like a radio without a dial.

Wide open, so everything floods in at once.

And sealed tight, so nothing escapes. Not even time,

Which should curl in on itself and loop around like smoke.

So that I might be sitting now beside my father

As he raises a lit match to the bowl of his pipe

For the first time in the winter of 1959.

4.

In those last scenes of Kubrick's *2001*
When Dave is whisked into the center of space,
Which unfurls in an aurora of orgasmic light
Before opening wide, like a jungle orchid
For a love-struck bee, then goes liquid,
Paint-in-water, and then gauze wafting out and off,
Before, finally, the night tide, luminescent
And vague, swirls in, and on and on. . . .

In those last scenes, as he floats
Above Jupiter's vast canyons and seas,
Over the lava strewn plains and mountains
Packed in ice, that whole time, he doesn't blink.
In his little ship, blind to what he rides, whisked
Across the wide-screen of unparcelled time,
Who knows what blazes through his mind?
Is it still his life he moves through, or does
That end at the end of what he can name?

On set, it's shot after shot till Kubrick is happy,
Then the costumes go back on their racks
And the great gleaming set goes black.

5.

When my father worked on the Hubble Telescope, he said
They operated like surgeons: scrubbed and sheathed
In papery green, the room a clean cold, and bright white.

He'd read Larry Niven at home, and drink scotch on the rocks,
His eyes exhausted and pink. These were the Reagan years,
When we lived with our finger on The Button and struggled

To view our enemies as children. My father spent whole seasons
Bowing before the oracle-eye, hungry for what it would find.
His face lit-up whenever anyone asked, and his arms would rise

As if he were weightless, perfectly at ease in the never-ending
Night of space. On the ground, we tied postcards to balloons
For peace. Prince Charles married Lady Di. Rock Hudson died.

We learned new words for things. The decade changed.

The first few pictures came back blurred, and I felt ashamed
For all the cheerful engineers, my father and his tribe. The second time,
The optics jibed. We saw to the edge of all there is—

So brutal and alive it seemed to comprehend us back.

ADRIENNE RICH

HUBBLE PHOTOGRAPHS: AFTER SAPPHO

for Jack Litewka

It should be the most desired sight of all
the person with whom you hope to live and die

walking into a room, turning to look at you, sight for sight
Should be yet I say there is something

more desirable: the ex-stasis of galaxies
so out from us there's no vocabulary

but mathematics and optics
equations letting sight pierce through time

into liberations, lacerations of light and dust
exposed like a body's cavity, violet green livid and venous, gorgeous

beyond good and evil as ever stained into dream
beyond remorse, disillusion, fear of death

or life, rage
for order, rage for destruction

—beyond this love which stirs
the air every time she walks into the room

These impersonae, however we call them
won't invade us as on movie screens

they are so old, so new, we are not to them
we look at them or don't from within the milky gauze

of our tilted gazing
but they don't look back and we cannot hurt them

WILLIAM WENTHE

A PHOTOGRAPH FROM THE HUBBLE TELESCOPE

These luminous clouds and whorls
of amethyst, jade, and coral
are transmitted down to earth
as a babble of data:
monochrome of linty gray
that arrives in computers
at NASA, gets filtered out,
and colored in with a menu
of splendid hues: the better
to illuminate the original
edge of the universe, and imagine
the most ancient of days.

In the same way, I suppose,
cathedrals' stained-glass windows
pieced ordinary light of the sun
into an old story of creation.
Perhaps there is no story
more ancient than our making
of images. Or more new:

I picture a darkened
chamber, and the glow
of monitor screen on the focused brow
of a technician—like torchlight
on the face of one who blows
powdered pigment through hollow bones
in caves of Lascaux.

STORY MUSGRAVE

COSMIC FIREFLIES

Floating in a spaceship,
Falling through my heaven,
Through epic altitudes,
And higher latitudes

Falling into sleep,
Drifting into dreams,
Cosmic crashes in my eye,
Cosmic flashes in my brain

Cosmic rays and Wilson clouds,
Clear my consciousness.
Memories of infinity,
Particles of eternity

Starlettes pierce my eyes,
In my brain fire flies.
Periods of light,
Punctuate my night

As astronaut Don Pettit explained on his blog in 2012, for astronauts outside Earth's atmosphere, "When a cosmic ray happens to pass through the retina it causes the rods and cones to fire, and you perceive a flash of light that is really not there. . . . The retina functions as a miniature Wilson cloud chamber where the recording of a cosmic ray is displayed by a trail left in its wake."

MARY JO SALTER

A KISS IN SPACE

That the picture
in *The Times* is a blur
is itself an accuracy. Where
this has happened is so remote
that clarity would misrepresent
not only distance but our feeling
about distance: just as
the first listeners at the telephone
were somehow reassured to hear
static that interfered with hearing
(funny word, *static*, that conveys
the atom's restlessness), we're
not even now—at the far end
of the century—entirely ready
to look to satellites for mere

resolution. When the *Mir*
invited the first American
astronaut to swim in the pool
of knowledge with Russians, he floated
exactly as he would have in space
stations of our own: no lane
to stay in, no line to determine
the deep end, Norman Thagard
hovered on the ceiling something
like an angel in a painting

(but done without the hard
outlines of Botticelli; more
    like a seraph's sonogram),
and turned to Yelena Kondakova
    as his cheek received her kiss.

        And in this
        too the blur made sense: a kiss
    so grave but gravity-free, untouched
by Eros but nevertheless
    out of the usual orbit, must
make a heart shift focus. The very
    grounding in culture (they gave him bread
and salt, as Grandmother would a guest
    at her dacha; and hung the Stars
and Stripes in a stiff crumple
    because it would not fall), the very
Russianness of the bear hugs was
    dizzily universal: for who
knows how to signal anything
    new without a ritual?

        Not the kitchen-table
        reader (child of the Cold War,
    of 3 x 5 cards, carbon copies,
and the manila folder), who takes a pair
    of scissors—as we do when the size
of some idea surprises—and clips
    this one into a rectangle
much like her piece of toast. There:
    it's saved, to think of later.
Yet it would be unfair
    to leave her looking smug; barely
a teenager when she watched, on
    her snowy TV screen, a man
seeming to walk on the moon, she's
    learned that some detail—

Virtual Reality or email,
something inexplicable and
unnatural—is always cropping up
for incorporation in what's human.
What ought to make it manageable,
and doesn't quite, is the thought
of humans devising it. She'll
remember Norman Thagard in June,
when the *Mir* (meaning Peace: but how
imagine this without agitation?)
docks with *Atlantis* (meaning
the island Plato mentioned first
and which, like him, did not disappear
without a splash), to shuttle
the traveler back home—or

to whatever Earth has become.

GWYNETH LEWIS

FROM "ZERO GRAVITY"

VIII

Thousands arrive when a bird's about to fly,
crowding the causeways. "Houston. Weather is a go
and counting." I pray for you as you lie
on your back facing upwards. A placard shows
local, Shuttle and universal time.
Numbers run out. Zero always comes.
"Main engines are gimballed" and I'm
not ready for this, but clouds of steam
billow out sideways and a sudden spark
lifts the rocket on a collective roar
that comes from inside us. With a sonic crack
the spaceship explodes to a flower of fire
on the scaffold's stamen. We sob and swear,
helpless, but we're lifting a sun
with our love's attention, we hear
the Shuttle's death rattle as it overcomes
its own weight with glory, setting car alarms
off in the Keys and then it's gone
out of this time zone, into the calm
of black and we've lost the lemon dawn
your vanishing made. At the viewing site
we pick oranges for your missing light.

XII

Only your eyesight can be used in space.
Now you've captured the telescope, nebulae
are birthmarks on your new-born face.
The sun's flare makes a Cyclops eye
on your visor. The new spectrograph
you've installed in the Hubble to replace the old
makes black holes leap closer, allows us to grasp
back in time through distance, to see stars unfold
in nuclear gardens, galaxies like sperm
swirled in water, rashes of young hot stars,
blood-clot catastrophes, febrile swarms
of stinging explosions. But what's far
doesn't stop hurting. Give me a gaze
that sees deep into systems through clouds of debris
to the heart's lone pulsar, let me be amazed
by the red shifts, the sheer luminosity
that plays all around us as we talk on the beach,
thinking there's nothing between us but speech.

XIV

There are great advantages to having been dead.
They say that Lazarus never laughed again,
but I doubt it. Your space suit was a shroud
and at night you slept in a catacomb,
posed like a statue. So, having been
out to infinity, you experienced the heat
and roar of re-entry, blood in the veins
then, like a baby, had to find your feet
under you, stagger with weight, learn to cope
again with gravity. Next came the tour
of five states with a stopover in Europe.
You let people touch you, told what you saw.
This counts as a death and a second birth
within one lifetime. This point of view
is radical, its fruit must be mirth
at one's own unimportance and now, although
you're famous, a "someone," you might want much less.
Your laughter's a longing for weightlessness.

Dedicated to the memory of Lewis's sister-in-law Jacqueline Badham (1944–97) and to commemorate the voyage of her cousin astronaut Joe Tanner and the crew of STS-82 to repair the Hubble Space Telescope (February 1997).

BETTY ADCOCK

FALLEN

The space shuttle Columbia *broke up over several East Texas counties, including sparsely populated San Augustine County, on the morning of February 1, 2003.*

Silver the winter morning, silver
the early sun downpouring
onto columns of pine and oak, miles
of birdsong-piercing silence silver
in the hour just before the rain;
and our shining myth oncoming, loosening
piecemeal overhead a ghastly charivari
in the high branches, mayhem broken
from the seared-off caul of cold space.

Imagine the torn, deer-haunted woods
where a severed foot still in its boot
was driven into mud. Imagine rags of flesh,
the heart found near a logging road,
the arm in underbrush, insignia beside
an upended helmet filling with icy rain.

Buzzards led the searchers—
       don't recoil—do
not imagine this a story to be tamed by naming
heroes who died for country and some further bourne
worth dying for.
      Don't imagine this as anything
beyond the old arc snapped, covenant entirely
broken, our ships no more than silver needles
trying the boundless haystacks of the stars.

Those shadow-stories people lived within
(when we were only hurt and poorly wise)
have hardened into nightmare: heaven
as fleshly destination, hell a fire
we make on earth where myth and science
change partners in the dance.

Only thin February light could plumb the deep
East Texas forests, men combing miles of underbrush
for the whole bloody puzzle, every shard
of failed metal and all the flesh it failed.
Among enormous trees, on a red clay road,
Chinquapin Baptist Church—chosen
beyond all prophecy and imagining—became
receiving station for the shattered dead.

Of course exhausted searchers didn't exhaust
that arboreous dark, its snarled thickets,
its hawk-sharpened air.
       Light-footed foxes live there,
wildcats, the invisible cougar, wild boar
winter-thin and hungry, and shuffling armadillos
better armored than the astronauts sent out
as latter knights to press
our argument with airlessness
and make a grail of the mirage our image is,
among the novas and the planetary shrugs.

Disarticulate as temples seized by jungle,
this journey too will disappear. For a while
a mangled piece of the spaceship's hull
swung high in a shagbark hickory,
        bell calling what faithful
                to the altar of the owl?

KEITH FLYNN

THE INVISIBLE BRIDGE

Inside the Space Station, amnesia's simple fog
is added to the litany of our growing physical
concerns. What are we without our memories?

Each meaningful success is littered with false starts,
lost in the gray mist as the great sun comes, and we
are stumbling about in our bulky suits, lunging

at every flicker of affection, caught in the gears
of the imagination's great harem, washed clean
of an earthbound past and its requisite boundaries.

Oblivious to recent mistakes, and insatiably curious,
the steaming brain rides on its spiral post like a train
gliding from station to station, gathering loaded

cars for its final climb. Behind us, the weight
of dreams slows our roll. Remember everything
and you have the record of each fugitive slight,

losing the ability to forgive. In the constant
process of regeneration, the logbooks fill up
with observations, and every 92 minutes,

another poem comes shining. We let our arms
drift out in the free gravity, and float past one
another silently, becoming the revolution

that is urged forward. Gathering clouds of carbon
migraine through the brittle space around us.
Since every second of our existence is expensive,

our peers are shot with excitement during each
mistake, filled with the terror of a loosened bolt.
We keep our shattered parts tucked out of sight.

We are filled with a beauty we cannot reflect,
and as we move from chamber to chamber,
we fly straight through without touching

the sides. Sometimes we drive with our knees,
and our big toes are calloused from pushing off.
Our eyesight is constantly getting worse,

so we listen with our whole beings, and forget
where we put the remote, the bandages, the keys.
We are moving ten times the speed of a bullet

and have no control. In the darkness we have
become the thing that the others fear most.
Unable to sleep and numb inside our own country,

we are lost in translation and free from familiars.
Invisible specters, holding between their hands
our most precious deconstructions, carve our

reflections into time's rough passage. Playing from
behind the practiced persona of lightly smoked glass,
we fling paper airplanes, we do lonely things.

ALISON HAWTHORNE DEMING

HOMELAND SECURITY

for Taylor Brorby

What is a day to the astronaut
floating two hundred miles
above Earth the space station
whirling fifteen and a half times
a day around the planet while
he drifts weightless as if unmoving
sipping meals from a plastic pouch?
Is that how it works keeping
everything contained
against the drift? His twin is
down there donating biometrics
to the database. What is a year
to them, their bones and hearts
and brains? That's what the
instruments want to know
or what we've taught them
to want. The space twin will
pay the higher price for his
unearthly habitation. Bodies
need gravity or some system

that simulates the magnetic pull
of mantle and core. He can see
home from a porthole in space
the planet from out here
sublime a blue and white
ball so tender it might be
made of glass just forming
at the tip of the glassblower's rod.

The Earth twin watches his brother
lift from the Cosmodrome.
Zero to seventeen thousand
in twelve minutes. "It feels like
the hand of God has come down
and grabbed you by the collar
and ripped you off the planet.
You know you're either going
to float in space or you're going
to be dead." What is Earth
to the astronaut? The exception
to emptiness. Boatloads of planets
lie further in the black concealment
of space. Best that we don't know
their voraciousness and need.
Our home we know is troubled
yet still in the heyday
of its experiment with life.
Thanks cyanobacteria
for your evolutionary largesse
the Great Oxygenation Event
that made us possible.

I'm writing this to find my way
into the fray over fracking—
wild card as it seems now that
I've gone so far out into space.
No one wants to hear again

about flaming water faucets
exploited towns and farms
heartland riddled with quakes
water poisoned and stuck back
in the ground to find its way home.
Space might be the only way
to see what kind of sky we need
and how the Great Carbonation Event
might be flipping the way
Earth does or doesn't do life.
We say "blue marble" we say
"Mother Earth" we say "home."
The astronaut says "Beautiful."
Earth from space says "Keep me."
The only thing that matters is
the carbon, so homeland
security means leave it
in the ground. Lock it up
with soldiers standing guard.
Shelter it with grassland and trees.

M A Y A   A N G E L O U

A BRAVE AND STARTLING TRUTH

Dedicated to the hope for peace, which lies, sometimes hidden, in every heart.

We, this people, on a small and lonely planet
Traveling through casual space
Past aloof stars, across the way of indifferent suns
To a destination where all signs tell us
It is possible and imperative that we learn
A brave and startling truth.

And when we come to it
To the day of peacemaking
When we release our fingers
From fists of hostility
When we come to it
When the curtain falls on the minstrel show of hate
And faces sooted with scorn are scrubbed clean
When battlefields and coliseum
No longer rake our unique and particular sons and daughters
Up with the bruised and bloody grass
To lay them in identical plots in foreign soil

When the rapacious storming of the churches
The screaming racket in the temples have ceased
When the pennants are waving gaily
When the banners of the world tremble
Stoutly in a good, clean breeze

When we come to it
When we let the rifles fall from our shoulders
And our children can dress their dolls in flags of truce
When land mines of death have been removed
And the aged can walk into evenings of peace
When religious ritual is not perfumed
By the incense of burning flesh
And childhood dreams are not kicked awake
By nightmares of sexual abuse

When we come to it
Then we will confess that not the Pyramids
With their stones set in mysterious perfection
Nor the Gardens of Babylon
Hanging as eternal beauty
In our collective memory
Not the Grand Canyon
Kindled into delicious color
By Western sunsets

Nor the Danube, flowing its blue soul into Europe
Not the sacred peak of Mount Fuji
Stretching to the Rising Sun
Neither Father Amazon nor Mother Mississippi
who, without favor,
Nurtures all creatures in their depths and on their shores
These are not the only wonders of the world

When we come to it
We, this people, on this minuscule globe
Who reach daily for the bomb, the blade, and the dagger
Yet who petition in the dark for tokens of peace
We, this people, on this mote of matter
In whose mouths abide cankerous words
Which challenge our very existence
Yet out of those same mouths
Can come songs of such exquisite sweetness

That the heart falters in its labor
And the body is quieted into awe

We, this people, on this small and drifting planet
Whose hands can strike with such abandon
That, in a twinkling, life is sapped from the living
Yet those same hands can touch with such healing,
irresistible tenderness,
That the haughty neck is happy to bow
And the proud back is glad to bend
Out of such chaos, of such contradiction
We learn that we are neither devils nor divines

When we come to it
We, this people, on this wayward, floating body
Created on this earth, of this earth
Have the power to fashion for this earth
A climate where every man and every woman
Can live freely without sanctimonious piety
Without crippling fear

When we come to it
We must confess that we are the possible
We are the miraculous, we are the true wonder of this world
That is when, and only when,
We come to it.

TO THE STARS, WITH DIFFICULTIES

FOR MANY readers, there is science fiction and there is poetry—separate genres doing different things. But science-fiction poetry is a subgenre within the larger "sci-fi" community (science-fiction writers hate that term, but the wider public uses it). This selection of poetry takes us from "yesterday's tomorrows" of, say, the *Star Trek* universe to contemporary visions of a future Mars in which humans are engineering its climate to sustain terrestrial life, then onward to indigenous imaginings of a wider cosmos as both a technological and spiritual home. And this is only a small sampling of mainstream poets, science-fiction authors better known for prose, and science-fiction poets who publish in journals specializing in that subgenre.

Some tensions—illuminating ones—may be apparent in the poems that follow. In mainstream literature—from avant-garde poetry to the realist novel—certain traits are valued, such as complex interiority and lyrical language. In science fiction, ideas and world-building are often foregrounded. This is a divide as old as the argument between H. G. Wells and Henry James on the function of the novel: Wells thought the novel was a vehicle for social change, James thought it was a foray into human lives. Of course, these things are not mutually exclusive, and especially after the 1960s New Wave in science fiction, literary technique and psychological complexity began to co-exist with ideas, world-building, and other science-fictional values such as the sublime. This was especially evident in novels, but the poems we include in this final section also capture this kind of unitary reading experience.

From Douglas Kearney's word-cloud visual poem "Afrofuturism" to an excerpt about the Martian landscape in Frederick Turner's book-length epic, *Genesis*, the poems here, we hope, complicate expectations and can offer both ideas and feelings. Mohja Kahf's "Hajar, First Woman on the Moon" brings the sweep of faith into a first-person narrative in which the speaker seeks some "anchor" to celestial flights. Peter Milne Greiner's "Hammerstone" muses on the costs of colonization, and they are more subtle than one might think. There are supernovae; strange experiences in time and space; ruminations on the other, on colonization and invasion, and on gardening entire planets to make them new and sustainable homes. There are broken hearts. And, finally, there are affirmations: the last two poems by Nikki Giovanni and Diane Ackerman acknowledge violence, change, and loss while imagining a way forward. The final lines of the book belong to Ackerman: "I am life, and life loves life."

Astronauts repeatedly have said that we should send poets to space. Here, they have so traveled, but perhaps it's time to take the call literally. At the cusp of what promises to be a newly invigorated era in spaceflight and exploration, one in which, perhaps ironically, wealthy elites may democratize access to low Earth orbit and other destinations—perhaps it is in this century that poets will write the first geosynchronous sonnets, the first villanelles from the tops of the Moon's Montes Apenninus.

We first went to space on words. Words are going there, too.

Christopher Cokinos

DOUGLAS KEARNEY

AFROFUTURISM

won't you let me take you on a ~~sea~~ cruise?

ROCKETS

so far ahead
it's behind us.
Moses tote her
raygun saying
moonwalk or git
disinigrated!

pharaohs go far away-o, no riding place down dere!

thrown up thrown up like they just don't care!

[eject]

what our antenna said we was bugged,
so us eyed the light up to light out.
whole of "...the place" blacked up so blacks out
this terra. o great gettin up launchin!
spacesuited Q.U.E.E.N.S. in foil to fly.
flightsuited kings sky around shinin.
zip zip zip off the planetation,
beyond the stairs to nigga heaven.

ROCKETS

it's an escape craft
from now&then
by way of then&soon.

"yeahyeahyeahyeah"
"yeahyeahyeahyeah"

MOONSHOTS

who you callin BUCK Rogers?!

it's the Where,
the When we go
" when the Call
gets no Response.
[do you read?
over.]

TAKE ME TO ~~YOUR LEADER~~
TAKE ME TO ~~YOUR LEADER~~
TAKE ME TO ~~YOUR LEADER~~
TAKE ME TO ~~YOUR LEADER~~
TAKE ME TO ~~YOUR LEADER~~
TAKE ME TO ~~YOUR LEADER~~
TAKE ME TO ~~YOUR LEADER~~
TAKE ME TO ~~YOUR LEADER~~
TAKE ME TO ~~YOUR LEADER~~
TAKE ME TO ~~YOUR LEADER~~
TAKE ME TO ~~YOUR LEADER~~
TAKE ME TO ~~YOUR LEADER~~
TAKE ME TO ~~YOUR LEADER~~
TAKE ME TO ~~YOUR LEADER~~
TAKE ME TO ~~YOUR LEADER~~
TAKE ME TO ~~YOUR LEADER~~
TAKE ME TO ~~YOUR LEADER~~

TAKE ME TO ■■■
TAKE ME TO ~~YOUR LEADER~~
TAKE ME TO ~~YOUR LEADER~~
TAKE ME TO ~~YOUR LEADER~~
TAKE ME TO ~~YOUR LEADER~~
TAKE ME TO ~~YOUR LEADER~~
TAKE ME TO ~~YOUR LEADER~~

MOONSHOTS

ASTROSHEEN®
REMY MARTIAN®
~~CADILLITE®~~
~~GALACTIC®~~
SPACEY ADAMS®

TAKE ME TO ■■■
TAKE ME TO ■■■
TAKE ME TO ~~YOUR LEADER~~
TAKE ME TO ~~YOUR LEADER~~
TAKE ME TO ~~YOUR LEADER~~

ROCKETS
"pilot...
"pilot...
"pilot...

are   we   *there*   yet?
are   we   *we*   yet?
are   we   *we*   there?
are there *we* there yet?
are we here *yet* there?
there,   there.

"NASA been good to us!
Dogonnit, I'm serious!"

who you callin StarBUCK?!

MOONSHOTS
"pilot...
"pilot...

MOHJA KAHF

HAJAR, FIRST WOMAN ON THE MOON

Abraham is a just dot now,
distant planet
Sarah's laughter floats by in globules
I grab, swallow one, laugh
I am alone in a space
no one else has ever inhabited

I'm not what I was before:
Not Sarah's Hajar,
nor Abraham's, not
a girl of Egypt anymore
Can't go back now

& I don't know
what else to be
What will anchor me?
I somersault like hiccups
There is too much noise on earth
to hear God there
In a life spent listening

to commandments, I never
had the luxury
of this lunar silence

Things whiz by. Djinns swing
from galactic chandeliers,
eavesdropping
Was that a ram?
Was that a lote tree?
I hear the beating of many wings
& someone being taken on a tour of heaven
Will these weightless shapes
be hewn into a cube
solid enough to anchor earth?
Did I touch that rock before?
Seven times?

LAURENCE GOLDSTEIN

FIRMAMENT ON HIGH

Once, we loved our sister satellite.
Desert Endymions hot to shoot off
we fashioned Cadillacs of ascent
to touch her dry Sea of Serenity.

What we thought heroic, wasn't.
Our old moon, Sagan says, is "boring,"
like police photos of gelid bodies
icepicked in the heart or neck.

Mars is a nastier myth, but
more *heimisch* for some latter-day
atom-energized Voyager
to lay by, the better to fly by

and finally, beyond Pluto, settle among
Eocene forms not yet imagined,
not humdrum, resourceful as rodents,
"intelligent life" we fondly call it,

meaning, smart enough to welcome *us*
their destiny, but smarter than us too,
having no need for cinema, jails
or moving vans to find out what they are.

FREDERICK TURNER

FROM *GENESIS: AN EPIC POEM*

A numb plain spread with stones. A weary steppe
All bleached to tired red with ultraviolet.
Soil crusted, sere; limonite, siderite.
Hard radiation in a waste of cold.
Rocks sucked dry by the near vacuum.
Stunned with the blank math of the albedo
The eye tries to make order of it, fails.
Whatever's here once fell from someplace else.
Sometimes a crag a foot high, or a mile;
Always the sagging tables of the craters,
The precise record of a mere collision.
And yet a stunted and abortive chemistry,
A backward travesty of life, proceeds:
Parched cirrus clouds move over the ejecta;
A hoarfrost forms upon the shadow sides;
Dark patches colonize the regolith;
Sometimes with a thin violence a sandstorm
Briefly makes shrieks of sound between the stones;
Rasps off their waists and edges, and falls silent.
Time here is cheap. A billion years can pass
Almost without a marker; if you bought
A century of Marstime in the scrip
And currency of Earth, you'd pay an hour
Or half an hour of cashable event.
It's really a young planet then, a bald
And mild mongoloid, a poor old cretin
Worth but a handful of Earth's golden summers.

And it was beautiful. Those who first walked there
Said it was fresh as the true feel of death,
As Kyoto earthen teaware, as the Outback;
As clean as is geometry, as bones.
To spoil this archetype, this innocence,
Was to incur a guilt whose only ease
Was beauty overwhelming to the loss,
Was a millennial drunkenness of life
That might forget its crime in ecstasy.
But it was not enough to reenact
The long sensualities of mother Earth,
To take on trust the roots of history;
They must be minatory, and exact
A last accounting of the failed balance
All the intestate dowager had left.
There must be new assumptions in the matrix,
New ratios, dimensions and arrays;
Beatrice finds her trope in simple mass,
The crazy lightness of all things here
Set, in a poetry that brewed delight,
Against the literal dimness of the light.

After the riot, then, of Earth diseases,
After mycosis, cometfall, the plague
And infestation of the weeds, the jungles
Of a lifeforce as fresh as it was vulgar,
The time came to prune and shape the flow.
On Mars all these fall slowly, dreamily:
Waterfalls, billowy, like the clawed waves
In Hiroshige prints of sudden storms.
Snow, in soft bales or volumes, scarcely more
Than bright concatenations of a vapor.
Rain, in fine drizzles, dropping by a cliff
Stained by the rocksprings and the clinging mosses.
Rivers and streams, whose wayward pressures thrust
More, by inertia, at their banks than beds,
And so can spread in braided flats and strands

To glittery sallow-marshes, quiet fens.
Ocean waves, swashy, horned, and globular,
Like the wave-scenery of an antique play,
(Bright blue horned friezes worked to and fro,
A fat-lipped leviathan, and a ship)
And then on Mars all these rise swifter, easier:
Smoke, which makes mushrooms in the wildest air;
Fountains, which tower and tower, whose very fall
Is caught up once again within the column
Of their slow and weighty rise; yes, fountains
Shall be the glory of our Martian gardens;
Flames, in like fashion, scarcely dance on Mars
So much as dart into the air, like spirits
Lately penned in earth but now set free.
And the warmed thermal plumes from open fields
Of ripened grass or stubble here make clouds
As tall as chefs' hats, stovepipes full of thunder.

The poets of the Earth refine the fuel—
The hot benzene of value culture burns
To power its subtle engines of desire—
From fossil liquors buried in the stone
Through ages of creation and decay.
They can afford to toss aside the raw,
And take for granted a world cooked and rich
With ancient custom, languages numberless
As layers of autumn leaves within the forest,
Nature itself grown conscious, turned upon
Itself to make its rings so intricate,
History fertile with its own grave-mould.
And so the poets' work is little more
Than cracking out the spirit they inherit
In the tall silver towers of poetry
To brew those essences, those volatiles,
Those aromatic esters, metaphor,
Image, trope and fugitive allusion.
Prodigals, they burn half that they use

To purify the rest; and they make little,
Only a froth or lace of ornament.
The poets of Mars must brew the very stuff
The Earth-poets burn as waste; must mate each word
With breeder's care, and dust the yellow pollen
Over the chosen stamen; graft the stem
To coarser stock, and train the line to sprout
Productive variation years ahead.
The poets of Mars must make the myths from scratch,
Invent the tunes, the jokes, the references;
They must be athletes of the dream, masters
Of the technology of inventive sleep,
Architects of the essential shades of mood.
What they inherit from the Earth, they earn,
Through sacrifice and trouble, and they breed
More than they are bequeathed. So Beatrice,
Taking into her hands her garden tools—
A dream of a Campanian burial,
A trope of lightness, and a wild new world—
Begins the cultivation of the void.

This garden: let it propagate itself,
Sustain itself, an arch-oeconomy
Dynamically balanced by the pull
Of matched antagonists, controlled and led
By a fine dance of feedbacks, asymptotic,
Cyclical, damping, even catastrophic.
Let there be forest fires to purge the ridges;
Let there be herbivores to mow the parkland,
And predators to cull their gene pools clean
And viruses to kill the carnivores
That sheep may safely graze. Each form of life
Shall feed upon the wastes of its convivors;
Let there be beetles and bacteria
And moulds and saprophytes to spin the wheel
Of nitrogen, corals and shells to turn
The great ratcheted cycle of the carbons;

Each biome—grassland, forest, littoral;
Benthic, pelagic; arctic, desert, alp—
Shall keep appointed bounds and yet be free.
Let the new species bud and multiply;
Let monsters speciate and radiate
And seize the niche that they themselves create;
Let some be smothered or extinguished; some,
Effete, exquisite—the trumpeter swan,
The rare orchid, the monoclone cheetah—
Cling to some microclimate or kind vale,
Eking survival for a clutch of genes.

BRENDAN CONSTANTINE

STILL LIFE ON MARS

It's taken everything to bring them here:
the peaches, grapes, oysters, the goblet
of wine, the table & cloth. Hardest of all
was keeping the snail alive 300 days,
hearty enough to survive two seconds
of posing.
　　　　We place it last, assuming the
other props will bear in the red air. They
don't. Before the snail dies (and it dies
in "One Mississippi") the peaches liquefy,
the grapes, too, the oysters implode like
novae. It's a massacre, right down to the
good linen & Château Latour.
　　　　　　　　We paint it
anyway, going slow to compensate for
our ridiculous gloves, stiff necks, the dim
light of the afternoon which is blue here.
It's worth all this to get it right. Indeed,
our life has never been so urgently shown.
How brief the fruit, the vintage & vessel.
How apt the snail, the half inch
of its glittering service.

KIM STANLEY ROBINSON

CANYON COLOR

In Lazuli Canyon, boating.
Sheet ice over shadowed stream
Crackling under our bow.
Stream grows wide, curves into sunlight:
A deep bend in the ancient channel.
Plumes of frost at every breath.
Endless rise of the red canyon,
Canyon in canyons, no end to them.
Black lines web rust sandstone:
Wind-carved boulder over us.
There, on a wet red beach—
Green moss, green sedge. Green.
Not nature, not culture: just Mars.
Western sky deep violet,
Two evening stars, one white one blue:
Venus, and the Earth.

WILL ALEXANDER

FROM "WATER ON NEW MARS"

"this doubled Mars
focused as strabismus
as purified eclectics
like the sulfur which roams in the Columbia Hills

the plateaus
like a glyph of wayward trilobites
which waver like the pull from irregular errata

my presence
being that primordial mineral flaring
that calligraphy which en-scars by pauses & flamings

a tumultuous scarring
like a quake from tumultuous kelvins
where the moons coalesce in waves
like burned or ellipsed volcanoes

such is the case of indefinite ruination
by ferment by withdrawal
where suns collapse & renew
& continue to de-exist

these being the figments where fauna commences
water being a quaking aural infinity
being a porous crystal in the flatlands
or an isometric crag in the Andes

this being Earth
& Mars
& New Mars
& being

this being a fabulous hydro-concision
like burning ice & marks
as imaginary ice steps on Rhea

which combines in blinding human ascendance
as thermotropism or touch
or the mind erupting from a pointless cortical breech

as trans-ocular ruin
I am astonishing spectre
a coursing solar day as darkness
baring boreal roots as proto-sorghum through spectra

to this degree a faultless thermal conjuration
a sightless phlogiston feeding
knowing doubled lightning bends
which flow in Sirenum Fossae

a blaze across a violet vascular field
a velocity alive in carbon astral water

being spell as blind electrical osmosis
being arc as ravine & chasm

New Mars
a blind & meandering energy as conundrum
as a magnetic platelet

minus itself in particles
being a glossary in Martian inaudia

where a partial sun expands
being a fabulatory vector
trans-active with vicinity"

ELIZABETH LINDSEY ROGERS

ARCADIA, MARS

To console myself, I wander
wing to wing in the orangery,
        slip between twisted limbs,
olives' silver and green. The air here
        whisks so convincingly, I can't believe
there's a rock partition keeping me
        safe from the pinked-out sky.

In Gethsemane—that ancient, other world—
        they say the Virgin Mary
is buried in a similar grove.
        They say any rock is agony. They say her grief
was deeper than those roots
        (the oldest known on Earth).

Our own carbon dates us. If I could cut
        myself open, you'd see rings
lapping more rings: my mother
        crying for her mother in the same
way her mother wept for hers.
        You'd see the silvery orbit,

where each life dissolved.
      But for now, I remain
human. I am a nesting doll for griefs.
      Even in utopia, there is suffering:
one sheep forced to walk
      the labyrinth, ensuring the grass
regenerates. And my young daughter,
      her legs thin as reeds,

chased and caught and pushed by
      the boys again. Her layers stripped away.
Not even the olive he wedged
      under her tongue
could hold her, clot those cries—
      these shepherds, they think of nothing but
what might wake this weak blue soil.

KYLE DARGAN

DEAR ECHO

I know the planet Earth is 'bout to explode.
Kind of hope that no one saves it.
We only grow from anguish.
—MAC MILLER

In the likely event of galactic calamity—
our sun's hydrogen reserves fused through,
the star-turned-red-giant bloating
as do our corpses—you will require flames.
Between the solar shockwave and Earth's
rattling—an opaque interval—you must
watch, but we people prior will have left
no crude fluid for ignition, for light,
having tapped this rock to gorge
our bellies to petroleum ache.
Perhaps you will have evolved—blood
supplemented with Edison and Tesla's
currents, half your body fed by generators
that slow cure your biomass or waste.
Maybe you will be self-luminous.
        But if you are still—like we,
like me—a mere meat pod fated to watch
Mercury and Venus engulfed, surely
you hold designs for an interplanetary ark.
Anticipate humanity's years spent

adrift in the dark liquor of space—lost
within hibernation and missing mother-
planet, further estranged from all
revelation of how we came to be.

From this unproven vantage point (inside
our history with no solid alpha), I claim to pity
your inherited task—to catalog the last
telluric pulse, close the case of "man" as now
known. But beneath my softened hide,
I'm envious. All of our missteps as shepherds,
all the graffiti eclipsing our souls, all of it
will cinder and you will view this erasure
from your Mars-bound barge. You will know
the phenomenon that is judgment, see it real time
as prophets allegedly witnessed. Sapiens will never
have beheld a clearer beacon to be reborn—

C. WADE BENTLEY

PALE BLUE

A supernova, caught in a light-
speed scream, appears frozen
in rictus—from Hubble, from
here. Henley's black night
is alive with energies light
and dark. A man in a lab
coat keeps his Higgs boson
close, and whispers up
at the sky: *Hey. Down*
here. Here are the first
colonists of Mars, climbing
Olympus in twilight, oxygen
humming as they wait
for Earthrise, radios gone
mute. At last, the blue eye
looks them over like a mother,
like a malamute, like a humpback
whale slowly rolling,
in the abysmal, unscrolling night.

MATTHEW OLZMANN

SPOCK AS A METAPHOR FOR THE CONSTRUCTION OF RACE DURING MY CHILDHOOD

Consider the mathematics of my German father.
The unconditional tears of my Filipino mother.

Call me Spock, but it was logic versus emotion
every day on Earth.

Out in space, there are over a million miles
between asteroids in an asteroid field.
It's pretty much impossible to hit one unless you actually aim for it.

Not so on *Star Trek*. There, they have to grit their teeth,
put their shields up, crash a couple times and assess the damage.

As a kid, I was amazed by the skill of those spacemen,
"skill" which I soon realized was nothing more than sheer incompetence.
Hitting an asteroid? *There's just no excuse for that.*

A modest revelation. But these revelations
strung themselves together, orbited the planet
in ways that messed with things like gravity and light.

It went like this: You knew you could fly
until your first attempt left you with two broken teeth.

You knew you were like all the other kids,
until your best friend said, *No, you're not.*

And he was right.
And in that moment, something shifted.
The galaxy became real, and in its realness, the asteroids
seemed so much closer than you thought.

You were half-alien, staring down an eternity
that was both limitless and dangerous
as a captain's voice boomed from above:
Brace for impact, we're going down.

BRYAN D. DIETRICH

FROM "THE ENGINEER"

IV.

So we go, boldly, back where we came before,
go blindly, proudly, in ships of steel, sterling ore,
go, go returning, past time itself, the core,
cavity, gravity, what drove us to this shore.
Matter driving matter to the heart of matter:
loss. Even Pound, poet, mad as a hatter,
knew the rest was dross. So we scatter
in these ships, these grails, each endless platter

a helping of us. And we reach, we send up flares,
catching something of the stars we seek, angels, unaware.
We push through all that emptiness, each portal, each tear,
knowing that we seek the end, what isn't there,
ships becoming stars themselves, something adorning
nothing. First star to the right and straight on 'til morning.

VII.

Our parents? Cold stone. Hot gas. A little DNA.
Where the gods, goddesses, some holy sobriquet?
Pater, *Madre*, Engineer, Intelligent Design?
Where Prime Directive? Beneficent, malign?
We do not wish to see ourselves as beast-bred, aping tools,
though no one has a problem being kin to molecules.
So take in hand, one, chemistry, and two, a teeming brain.
Mix in dreams of Eden in an interstellar rain.

Dilithium and nacelles we'll need. Perhaps a shuttlecraft.
But none of this can work without a soul to man the raft.
We've needed one, an Engineer, to make us, take us up.
Our fear is what has brought us here, oh Captain. Breaking up.
Yes, fears are what has brought us here, captains of the night,
sons of suns, engineers, dust clouds calving light.

'ANNAH SOBELMAN

POSSIBLE MARGINS OF ERROR AND VARIATION IN THE MATTER STREAM

Since he can't find sleep anymore he paces on deck wondering

about what happened to him in the transporter stream when he was beamed
    up

        from the other location. *Occasionally very*
bright, and marathon soft

or stiff as frozen stars, even what they call the wastes

        are pretty. Matter

from the streamer might have been accidentally beamed aboard but why

        does he feel
so strange? *There's no margin*

for error, one atom off and poof you're gone,
        he'd initially argued not

        wanting
to be so unraveled

and raveled back up again like that. *Tell*

me about your heart. And sure enough the dead body of his predecessor

lies there stiff
  like the slipknot of proof caught in

the broken fever of matter. *Could all this be equivalent to jazz?* Exploding

  the joints
of cerebral synapses, the old religion. *Does*

  the singeing of half-lives sing? He feels
his throat, his arm, his chest. Becomes thirstier than a bird. Ambles

past the pulsing big windows of

  space, stars silky with their trust-me implications, and when he asks
    the

computer stress reduction program it gives him in the accurate voice

  of the female *more*
birds beside the salty

  waves. Calm, calm,

he also intones as if to create a temporary home, *what* are *these variations*
    that keep whistling through

  the monster
blood so fast, so brave

if only I could catch catch catch them? Could he have imagined it,

they wonder? *Spatial relationships are all*
    distorted in the matter

stream. What marked his right arm like that? *Turned to fluorescent*

confetti stored in fluctuating, windy

currency, detailed,

immense. Different, I tell you, than the sirens he was no longer groping

towards. *Matter*
matter matter, what

are these discrete
caches of light? The biofilter,

you see, could not distinguish between the molecules and the
something
which looked animal and even mythological

to him, part leopard part snake. *He pushed molecular dispersion way past the*
integrity

point almost
just before the human

patterns began starting to degrade. They

did not expect it. What made him begin to start singing like that?

Refers to "Realm of Fear" (1992), a sixth-season episode of Star Trek: The Next Generation, *in which Lieutenant Reginald Barclay must confront his fear of the transporter to help search for the missing crew of the USS Yosemite. Barclay's paranoia leads to the rescue of the missing crew members, who turn out to be trapped in the transporter's matter stream.*

RAE ARMANTROUT

NEXT GENERATIONS

1

But, on "Star Trek," we *aren't* the Borg,

the aggressive conglomerate,

each member part humanoid, part

machine, bent on assimilating

foreign cultures. In fact,

we destroy their ship,

night after night,

in preparation for sleep.

2

We sense something's wrong

when our ideal selves

look like contract players.

The captain plays what's left

of believable authority

as a Shakespearean actor.

The rest are there to show surprise

each time

the invading cube appears—

until any response seems stupid.

But we forgive them.

We've made camp

in the glitch

ENDOR (DISAMBIGUATION)

In a hut in the Star Wars universe,
on the forest moon of Endor,
a creature carefully draws a map
of things connected to other things.

The creature draws a road between
two worlds, because one Elvish name
for Tolkien's Middle-earth is also
this forest moon or the planet
the forest moon orbits—
on this point the Star Wars universe is unclear.

Maybe our universe has a finite number
of times you can summon the dead
so we've begun to repeat ourselves.

Endor, ancient Canaanite village,
home of the witch who conjured Samuel.
Endor, Palestinian village,
depopulated. Endor, Israeli kibbutz.
Endor, the most successful town
in *Dragon Quest IV: Chapters of the Chosen.*

So who can blame the Israelite king
for wanting his best prophet
back from the land of the dead?

Who can blame the witch,
who only did what was asked of her?
Endor, forest moon, home place.

There were so many worlds
I longed to visit as a child,
where the creatures, the citizens,
would line up along the street
to say, *Welcome friend, welcome stranger.*

PETER VIERECK

SPACE-WANDERER'S HOMECOMING

After eight thousand years among the stars
Nostalgia—suddenly—for August
Tugged me like guilt through half a cosmos
Back to a planet sweet as canebrake.
Where winds have plumes and plumes have throats,
Where pictures
Like "blue" and "south" can break your heart with hints.

After a mere eight flickers nothing changed there
Among the birds, still just as blazing,
Among the lilt of leaves on rivers.
The heartbreak of the south and blue.
The canebrake-sweet of August night;
No change till
I, changeling, asked the natives: "Oh my people,

"After eight cycles, how is this you greet me?
Where is my horse? Where is my harp?
Why are the drums of goat-skin silent?
Spin my abyss of resin-wine;
Drape me my coat of prophecy;
My name is—."
Forgot it, I forgot it, the name "man."

C. S. E. COONEY

DOGSTAR MEN

All the men I might have loved
Have gone to Sirius

Sirius, the Dogstar
The Dreadstar of Summer
That Cranberry Bog, that Red Lamp District
Promising Scarlet Women, Scarlet Waves of Grain
A Wine-Stained Sea

My lovely men are gone
Leaving their braids behind them

They have left their braids
But have taken the veins of their wrists
Their bony faces and transparent fingers
Their cigarettes
Even the moist taunt of their throats
They have stolen away
Forsaking everything
To be happy on Sirius

O Sirius, your houses are made
Of bougainvillea leaves
Your rain is pink and balsamic
There is bloodsoup to eat, and dragons
And everyone is a surgeon

Like Magellan before them
My men have circumnavigated mystery
Without me

PETER MILNE GREINER

HAMMERSTONE

There is poetry in giving up one's vision by lengthening it, distending it out past death, past recognizability. When I turned thirty I left MIT and gave up on exoplanets, on Sagan, on extraterrestrial relics hanging in the dark like mobiles, Ozymandian and indifferent, their promises of sea change and revelation scattered out there in the wide, deaf galactic susurrus. I became an economist. I retired from speculation and became a speculator. A prospector. I stopped looking for big things far away. Cosmology is really just the study of scale. There's still something of that in my work. The Belt is my Cosmos, though some call it a driveway, a grind, a cul-de-sac. It's how I made my first trillion. I never thought I would hate space. But I do. When I turned sixty they needed me up there and, as always, I acquiesced. I had given ten years here and there to other things I didn't want before. Why not do it again, I mused, without a question mark so much as an ellipsis, the ellipsis in which all dreamers' schemes are fated to wordlessly pend, the ellipsis that is my totem. All the money in the world, and I have a lot of it, can't buy reliable gravity or even a nice rug, and those are really the only things I wanted for my "office." I haven't even told you what I do now, have I? I know where all the asteroids are. I pick them out, I reel them in, knap them down, suck them dry, and I work in orbit in January and February, which is very hard on my knee. Sometimes—right now is one of those times—I imagine skittering out of the Lagrange point in my preposterous monocle of an observatory and beading away into space like lymph. Adrift, starving myself as monks do, I would lower my metabolism and heart rate and self to just above zero, and very slowly, over the course of millennia, make my way to one of the Earth analogues. I'm an ambassador at heart: my true missed calling. I see the Belt as something Earthly still; roots and tubers floating through a vacuum-black consommé. What some see as mountains of platinum, nickel, and water ice, I see as radish, salsify, yuka. I'm a gatherer. Somewhere down the line my efforts will segue aloofly into the vision I've had—for myself and for the civilization I represent and participate in less and less. It's like my vision and I are moving farther and farther apart the closer I get to it, the more I age, the deeper into space's cramped cave I wriggle. That's what it feels like in here, too. It's like I've shaped the stone into plastic, woven baskets from wires, melted the mountain down to alerts and interfaces. I found a very good rock today. It's far. The op will take years. I'm leaving the giant beet to someone special in my will, in case I die. It's the biggest thing anyone has ever given to anyone else. I'm dispatching the drones tomorrow. They are the spears I hurl into each eye of the wooly rhinoceros. When it arrives in Earth orbit I will share it with my kin. I will look out across the savannah of stars and taste blood.

TAWAHUM JUSTIN BIGE

STAR LODGE

astral   project
Indigenous futurism
        cyberpunk spacecraft

moonrock
        ambush
firing laser projectiles
        from
electro-bow

robots programmed with a connection
to creation   transmitting radio signals
on reciprocation

this is not a   second chance
but an   extension
cord   umbilical
                    unbiblical

                    Indigenous resurgence
                        across solar systems
                    traditional hunting grounds
                            across mercury
                    living off interplanetary

                    land

space seal hunting on pluto
Elders watching
ceres   chiron   lilith
curving around the sun
                in ovoids
recording interstellar
winter solstice
        to spring equinox
            and summer to
                    aroma of crushed leaves musty
                        sage and sweetgrass burning
                            as the gas of venus

                        put down tobacco
                    in orbit around saturn
                    before pulling debris away
            to build our wigwams

        obviously
        space Dene
        live between
uranus   and   neptune
        the planetary north

Cree Sundances   on mercury
    a new kind of sacrifice
        and one hell
            of a tan

                god be damned
                    we ain't alone
out here

                    after all
            just us long-standing hybrids
        intergalactic chimeras
    mixed matched
    and starsilk stacked
weaved and stitched

                    dnb pow wow drum
echoes   across   galaxies
        beating the heart
            of these ancient
                            imaginations

                    our bodies reflect the land
                    so bring me to jupiter
                        to see how noxious
                            and eternal storms
                                    shape
                            evolution

                    herd buffalo
                    across dusty orange plains
                    mars

                    Raven and Coyote emerge
                        out of saturn
                        to rearrange the lovers
                            orbiting   jupiter
                    replacing   those   star stories
                with   something   fitting
                        our   expanding   breath

                        i can see it now
                        whether the sky is blue
in daytime
            or starshine
                        i continue to dream
with venus-powered heart
                            and imagination energized
by neptune

out here

        travelling

LO KWA MEI-EN

PASTORAL FOR COLONIAL CANDIDACY

Zilch, said the doctor of my amygdala.
You need help. I did not say, *You had one fucking job*. I have a futurist's job,
x-ray doors, locks, and a mechanism heroic, a mechanic
who shows up for what was long since determined—
Vicarious living, he said, *is the center of the black hole
united nations built the equation to build. I have seen the colonists off
to this center, and was almost agog.*
So the absence of love is now the ground I would flee, the very earth . . .
Regarding my health, a quality not nothing! Psi over psi,
quantities of humor balanced on a verge like the belly of a J—
Perhaps, but your heart, he said. *The sky of me is working art, sick
on need*, I did not say, *a velveteen chasm and murderous chill.
Necks crane to take the nothing in and hunt the seam
marrying my warring parts in the torrid light of the moon . . .*
Lariat of belonging, I see you rope the colonists to a vertigo,
keening. My doctor's decision is the needle-tip
jostling an addict who swore he would refuse the tranq.
I said, *I have not yet begun to live*. I said it, but have never
hated a thing like I hate life. This mess. This horizon a pink collar on excess.
God's affidavit with the stars; the perfection of a gunshot

flushing the body of intent. *Doctor*, I said, *until thou*
endearest thine self to my absence of the fucking balance of a V,
diagnose not the margin of my center. There are things you do not know.
Cool, glinting green waits for me on each cosmic continent this appetite's pox
blankets with ash, and—*God, man*, the doctor cried, *do you see the boy*
asleep as the sky burns? The blessèd zero of him, and on his chin, a bit of fuzz?

NARU DAMES SUNDAR

ORIGAMI CRANE /
LIGHT-DEFYING SPACESHIP

Origami crane with big spaceship dreams,
Crisp Japanese paper painted in peonies
Creased into feather and bone and
The absence of feet, with soft bloated corners.
(Because the boy
    with his toffee-sticky fat fingers
       was impatient)

But mountain and valley are not fusion torii
And the field of peonies does not limn starlight.
Marooned on the faded mahogany table
With no hope of sky, dreaming of
Astrogation, nebulae, and the gleam of suns

In its deep paper heart, lantern-bright,
Folds turn into spars, and valleys into engines
And origami crane skitters across galaxies.

Light-defying spaceship with tiny paper dreams,

City-long spars of iron painted in somber gray,
Tessellated into hull and spine and
Geometries sculpted by dead mathematicians.
(Because shipwrights
with their coffee-stained hands
abjure ornament and gilt)

But bones of steel are not creases like blades,

And ten clicks of engine do not fit on a single page.
Adrift in the empty, beyond well and orbit,
With no hope of simple pleasures, dreaming of
Mountain, valley, edge and fold.

In its sad metal-clad heart, molten as suns,

Spars turn to folds, and engines into valleys
And light-defying spaceship collapses into a

Tiny yellowed crane, peonies faded,

On a shipwright's table.

SARAH BLAKE

NEUTRON STAR

At the museum, I stand on a scale that tells me how much I'd weigh on a
  neutron star. (Trillions of pounds.)
I could walk the 20 miles around it in a day or two, except
not at that weight. Wherever I ended up on the star, that'd be it for me.

And also I'd be burned up faster than you can tut your tongue.
And also I'd be imploding from the pressure.

I guess I'd be a mess of ash pulled quickly to the surface.
And then that'd keep burning.

Neutron stars are the densest, but that's only because the ones with more
  mass turned into black holes.
I'd rather not say those don't exist, that those anti-exist. I'd rather say
those are still dense stars, just more dense, more dense.

If we figure out teleportation, I can imagine the tests.
We set up a camera feed off a satellite, and we send a mannequin in a new
  suit up there,
and we watch our equipment fail, and the mannequin disappears in a sort
  of explosion, and we try again.

And once the mannequin holds up, we send a doll full of fluid. Then an
   animal.
Then a bigger animal. And lots of them die despite our precautions. But
   we figure it out.
And someone stands on the neutron star eventually.

Someone feels like trillions of pounds in a suit that's counteracting feeling
   like trillions of pounds
and rotating rapidly through the universe. And while they're gone one of
   the animals
that's returned safely dies from a complication no one and everyone
   foresaw.

And it's ok because the person standing on the neutron star expected that.
And it's ok because they don't believe in living on Earth anymore.

They don't believe in it at all.

NIKKI GIOVANNI

QUILTING THE BLACK-EYED PEA

(We're Going to Mars)

We're going to Mars for the same reason Marco Polo rocketed
to China
for the same reason Columbus trimmed
his sails on a dream of spices
for the very same reason Shackleton
was enchanted with penguins
for the reason we fall in love
It's the only adventure

We're going to Mars because Peary couldn't go to the North
Pole without Matthew Henson
because Chicago couldn't be a city
without Jean Baptiste Du Sable
because George Washington Carver and
his peanut were the right partners for
Booker T.
It's a life seeking thing

We're going to Mars because whatever is wrong with us will not
get right with us so we journey forth

carrying the same baggage
but every now and then leaving
one little bitty thing behind:
maybe drop torturing Hunchbacks here;
maybe drop lynching Billy Budd there;
maybe not whipping Uncle Tom to death;
maybe resisting global war.

One day looking for prejudice to slip. . . . . . .one day looking for hatred to tumble by the wayside. . . . . . .one day maybe the whole community will no longer be vested in who sleeps with whom. . . . . . .maybe one day the Jewish community will be at rest. . . . . . .the Christian community will be content. . . . . . .the Muslim community will be at peace. . . . . . .and all the rest of us will get great meals at Holydays and learn new songs and sing in harmony

We're going to Mars   because it gives us a reason to change
If Mars came here   it would be ugly
                nations would band together to hunt down
                    and kill Martians
                and being the stupid undeserving life forms
                    that we are
                we would also hunt down and kill
                    what would be termed
                Martian Sympathizers
                As if the *Fugitive Slave Law* wasn't
                    bad enough then
                As if the so-called *War on Terrorism*
                    isn't pitiful Now

When do we learn and what does it take to teach us things
  cannot be:
                What we want
                When we want
                As we want
            Other people have ideas and inputs
            And why won't they leave Rap Brown alone
The future is ours to take

We're going to Mars because we have the hardware to do it . . .

                         we have

                      Rockets and fuel and money and stuff

                      and the only

                      Reason NASA is holding back is they

                      don't know

                      If what they send out will be what they

                      get back

So let me slow this down;

Mars is 1 year of travel to get there. . . . . . .

       plus 1 year of living on Mars. . . . . . .

       plus 1 year to return to Earth. . . . .

       = 3 years of Earthlings being in a tight space going to an unknown place with an unsure welcome awaiting them . . . tired muscles . . . unknown and unusual foods . . . harsh conditions . . . and no known landmarks to keep them human . . . only a hope and a prayer that they will be shadowed beneath a benign hand and there is no historical precedent for that except this:

The trip to Mars can only be understood through Black Americans
I say, the trip to Mars can only be understood through Black Americans

The people who were captured and enslaved immediately recognized the men who chained and whipped them and herded them into ships so tightly packed there was no room to turn . . . no privacy to respect . . . no tears to fall without landing on another . . . were not kind and gentle and concerned for the state of their souls . . . no . . . the men with whips and chains were understood to be killers . . . feared to be cannibals . . . known to be sexual predators . . . The captured knew they were in trouble . . . in an unknown place . . . without communicable abilities with a violent and capricious species . . .
But they could look out and still see signs of Home

      they could still smell the sweetness in the air

      they could see the clouds floating above the land they loved

But there reached a point where the captured could not only not look back

      they had no idea which way "back" might be

      there was nothing in the middle of the deep blue water to

indicate which way home might be and it was that
moment . . . when a decision had to be made:
> Do they continue forward with a resolve to see
> this thing through or do they embrace the waters
> and find another world

In the belly of the ship a moan was heard . . . and someone
picked up the moan . . . and a song was raised . . . and that song
would offer comfort . . . and hope . . . and tell the story . . .

When we go to Mars. . . . . .it's the same thing. . . .it's Middle
  Passage
When the rocket red glares the astronauts will be able to see
themselves pull away from Earth . . . as the ship goes deeper
they will see a sparkle of blue . . . and then one day not only will
they not see Earth . . . they won't know which way to look . . .
and that is why NASA needs to call Black America

They need to ask us: How did you calm your fears . . . . How
were you able to decide you were human even when everything
said you were not . . . How did you find the comfort in the face
of the improbable to make the world you came to your world . . .
How was your soul able to look back and wonder

And we will tell them what to do: To successfully go to Mars
and back you will need a song . . . take some Billie Holiday for
the sad days and some Charlie Parker for the happy ones but
always keep at least one good Spiritual for comfort . . . You
will need a slice or two of meatloaf and if you can manage it
some fried chicken in a shoebox with a nice moist lemon pound
cake . . . a bottle of beer because no one should go that far with-
out a beer and maybe a six-pack so that if there is life on Mars
you can share . . . Popcorn for the celebration when you land
while you wait on your land legs to kick in . . . and as you climb
down the ladder from your spaceship to the Martian surface . . .
look to your left . . . and there you'll see a smiling community
quilting a black-eyed pea . . . watching you descend

DIANE ACKERMAN

ODE TO THE ALIEN

Beast, I've known you
in all love's countries, in a baby's face
        knotted like walnut meat,
                in the crippled obbligato
        of a polio-stricken friend,
in my father's eyes
        pouchy as two marsupials,
                in the grizzly radiance
of a winter sunset, in my lover's arm
        veined like the Blue Ridge Mountains.
To me, you are beautiful
                until proven ugly.

Anyway, I'm no cosmic royalty
either: I'm a bastard of matter
        descended from countless rapes
                and invasions
        of cell upon cell upon cell.
I crawled out of slime;
        I swung through the jungles
                of Madagascar;

I drew wildebeest on the caves at Lascaux;
 I lived a grim life
 hunting peccary and maize
in some godforsaken mudhole in the veldt.

 I may squeal
 from the pointy terror of a wasp,
or shun the breezy rhetoric
 of a fire;
but, whatever your form, gait, or healing,
 you are no beast to me,
I who am less than a heart-flutter
 from the brute,
 I who have been beastly so long.
Like me, you are that pool
 of quicksilver in the mist,
 fluid, shimmery, fleeing, called life.

 And life, full of pratfall and poise,
 life where a bit of frost
one morning can turn barbed wire
 into a string of stars,
 life aromatic with red-hot pizazz
drumming ha-cha-cha
 through every blurt, nub, sag,
 pang, twitch, war, bloom of it,
life as unlikely as a pelican, or a thunderclap,
 life's our tour of duty
 on our far-flung planets,
 our cage, our dole, our reverie.

 Have you arts?
 Do waves dash over your brain
 like tide along a rocky coast?
Does your moon slide
 into the night's back pocket,
 just full when it begins to wane,

so that all joy seems interim?
                Are you flummoxed by that millpond,
deep within the atom, rippling out to every star?
                   Even if your blood is quarried,
I pray you well,
      and hope my prayer your tonic.

                I sit at my desk now
                      like a tiny proprietor,
a cottage industry in every cell.
     Diversity is my middle name.
My blood runs laps;
            I doubt yours does,
                but we share an abstract fever
                      called thought,
a common swelter of a sun.
So, Beast, pause a moment,
               you are welcome here.
            I am life, and life loves life.

BIBLIOGRAPHY

The following are some of the sources that informed the section headnotes.

Burrows, William E. *This New Ocean: The Story of the First Space Age*. Random House, 1998.

Chaikin, Andrew. *A Man on the Moon: The Voyages of the Apollo Astronauts*. Penguin, 1994.

Dean, Margaret Lazarus. *Leaving Orbit: Notes from the Last Days of American Spaceflight*. Graywolf Press, 2015.

Launius, Roger D. *The Smithsonian History of Space Exploration: From the Ancient World to the Extraterrestrial Future*. Smithsonian Books, 2018.

Logsdon, John. *After Apollo? Richard Nixon and the American Space Program*. Palgrave Macmillan, 2015.

———. *Ronald Reagan and the Space Frontier*. Palgrave Macmillan, 2019.

———. *The Penguin Book of Outer Space Exploration*. Penguin Classics, 2018.

Maher, Neil M. *Apollo in the Age of Aquarius*. Harvard University Press, 2017.

McCurdy, Howard E. *Space and the American Imagination*. Smithsonian Institution Press, 1997.

McDougall, Walter A. *. . . The Heavens and the Earth: A Political History of the Space Age*. Basic Books, 1985.

Michigan Quarterly Review. "The Moon Landing and its Aftermath." Volume 18, number 2, Spring 1979.

Olsen, Karen Yelena, editor. *On the Wing: American Poems of Air and Space Flight*. University of Iowa Press, 2005.

Phillips, Robert, editor. *Moonstruck: An Anthology of Lunar Poetry*. The Vanguard Press, 1974.

Pyne, Stephen J. *Voyager: Seeking Newer Worlds in the Third Great Age of Discovery.* Viking, 2010.

Smith, Andrew. *Moondust: In Search of the Men Who Fell to Earth.* Fourth Estate, 2005.

Shetterly, Margot Lee. *Hidden Figures: The American Dream and the Untold Story of the Black Women Mathematicians Who Helped Win the Space Race.* William Morrow, 2016.

Stern, Alan, and David Grinspoon. *Chasing New Horizons: Inside the Epic First Mission to Pluto.* Picador, 2018.

Vas Dias, Robert, editor. *Inside Outer Space: New Poems of the Space Age.* Anchor Books, 1970.

Weber, Ronald. *Seeing Earth: Literary Responses to Space Exploration.* Ohio University Press, 1985.

Weitekamp, Margaret A. *Right Stuff, Wrong Sex: America's First Women in Space Program.* Johns Hopkins University Press, 2005.

BIOGRAPHICAL NOTES

Julie Swarstad Johnson is the author of the poetry collection *Pennsylvania Furnace* (2019), editor's choice selection for the Unicorn Press First Book Series, as well as the chapbooks *Orchard Light* (2020) and *Jumping the Pit* (2015). She has been the recipient of a grant from the Arizona Commission on the Arts and has served as Artist in Residence at Gettysburg National Military Park. She lives in Tucson and works at the University of Arizona Poetry Center.

Christopher Cokinos is the author of *Hope Is the Thing with Feathers: A Personal Chronicle of Vanished Birds* (2000) and *The Fallen Sky: An Intimate History of Shooting Stars* (2009). His essay collection, *Bodies, of the Holocene*, was published by Truman, and *The Underneath* was winner of the 2016 New American Poetry Prize. With Eric Magrane, he is co-editor of *The Sonoran Desert: A Literary Field Guide* (University of Arizona Press, 2016).

John M. Logsdon is Professor Emeritus of Political Science and International Affairs at George Washington University's Elliott School of International Affairs. He was the founder in 1987 and long-time director of GW's Space Policy Institute. His recent books include *John F. Kennedy and the Race to the Moon* (2010), *After Apollo? Richard Nixon and the American Space Program* (2015), and *Ronald Reagan and the Space Frontier* (2019).

Poet, essayist, and naturalist **Diane Ackerman** is the author of two dozen highly acclaimed works of nonfiction and poetry, including *The Zookeeper's Wife* (2007) and *A Natural History of the Senses* (1990). Her works have been recognized as finalists for the Pulitzer Prize and National Book Critics Circle Award and have been adapted as a feature film and a PBS television series.

Betty Adcock is the author of eight books of poetry, including her most recent, *Rough Fugue* (2017). She has been the recipient of two Pushcart Prizes, a Guggenheim Fellowship, and many other honors. She taught for twenty years at Meredith College and for ten years at the Warren Wilson College MFA Program for Writers.

Poet, educator, memoirist, scholar, and arts activist **Elizabeth Alexander** is president of the Andrew W. Mellon Foundation. She is a chancellor of the Academy of American Poets, serves on the Pulitzer Prize Board, and co-designed the Art for Justice Fund. She is author or co-author of fourteen books, most recently a memoir, *The Light of the World*, which was a finalist for the Pulitzer Prize in 2015.

Will Alexander is a poet, aphorist, essayist, playwright, novelist, visual artist, and pianist; he has authored more than thirty books and chapbooks. His work has been recognized with a Whiting Fellowship for Poetry, and he is a Jackson Poetry Prize winner and an American Book Award winner.

Maya Angelou (1928–2014) was a major poet and writer of the twentieth century, author of the iconic *I Know Why the Caged Bird Sings* (1969) and many other works of poetry, essays, and autobiography. A civil-rights activist, former dancer, director, and actress, Angelou gave voice to the experiences of African Americans, especially African American women, and was the first presidential inaugural poet, in 1993, since Robert Frost in 1961.

Rae Armantrout is the author of fourteen books of poetry, including *Versed*, which received the 2010 Pulitzer Prize for Poetry as well as the National Book Critics Circle Award. Her writing has additionally been recognized with awards from the Guggenheim Foundation, the Fund for Poetry, and the California Arts Council.

W. H. Auden (1907–73) is perhaps best known for his poem "Musée des Beaux Arts." The English poet, who later moved to the United States, was a towering figure in modern literature, renowned for his linguistic skill and moralistic impulses. He won the Pulitzer Prize for Poetry in 1948 for *The Age of Anxiety*.

Dan Beachy-Quick is the author or co-author of fourteen books of poetry, exploratory prose, and fiction, including his most recent book of poetry, *gentlessness* (2015). His work has been supported by the Lannan Foundation, and he has taught at the School of the Art Institute of Chicago and Colorado State University.

Alyse Bensel is the author of *Rare Wondrous Things* (2020), a poetic biography of Maria Sibylla Merian. She is also the author of three poetry chapbooks, including her most recent, *Lies to Tell the Body* (2018). She is an assistant professor of English at Brevard College, where she directs the Looking Glass Rock Writers' Conference.

C. Wade Bentley teaches and writes in Salt Lake City. His poems have been published or are forthcoming in many journals, including *Cimarron Review*, *Best New Poets*, *Rattle*, *Poetry Daily*, and *Poetry Northwest*. A full-length collection of his poems, *What Is Mine*, was published in 2015.

Jessica Rae Bergamino is the author of *Unmanned*, winner of the 2017 Noemi Press Book Award for Poetry, as well as three chapbooks. Individual poems have appeared in publications such as *Third Coast*, *Black Warrior Review*, *The Journal*, and *Gulf Coast*. She is a doctoral candidate in Literature and Creative Writing at the University of Utah, and lives in Seattle.

Tawahum Justin Bige is a Łutselk'e Dene and Plains Cree Two-Spirit and Nonbinary poet who resides on unceded Musqueam, Tsleil-Waututh, and Squamish territory colonially known as Vancouver. Tawahum has performed on stages including the Talking Stick Festival and Verses Festival of Words. Their debut poetry collection, *Political & Personal*, is forthcoming from Metatron Press.

Sarah Blake is the recipient of a Literature Fellowship from the National Endowment for the Arts. She is the author of two collections of poetry, *Mr. West* (2015) and *Let's Not Live on Earth* (2018), and a novel, *Naamah* (2019). She lives near Philadelphia.

Bruce Bond is the author of several poetry collections, including *Blackout Starlight: New and Selected Poems 1997–2015*. A jazz and classical guitarist, Bond teaches English at the University of North Texas, where he is the poetry editor for *American Literary Review*.

Ray Bradbury (1920–2012) changed the course of science fiction in the 1950s with works such as *The Martian Chronicles* (1950) and *Fahrenheit 451* (1953), giving the genre literary credibility through his elevated language and range of cultural reference. Over his long career, Bradbury wrote many novels, short-story collections, and essays. He is less known as a poet, but in his best work he achieves an alchemy between his spiritual longing and mythic lyricism.

Gabrielle Calvocoressi is the author of *Rocket Fantastic* (2017), *Apocalyptic Swing* (2009), and *The Last Time I Saw Amelia Earhart* (2005). A recipient of numerous awards and fellowships, Calvocoressi serves as an editor at large at *Los Angeles Review of Books* and poetry editor at *Southern Cultures* and teaches at the University of North Carolina at Chapel Hill.

Heather Christle is the author of *The Crying Book* (2019), as well as four poetry collections, including her most recent, *Heliopause* (2015). She is an assistant professor of creative writing at Emory University and lives in Decatur, Georgia.

David Clewell has published eight collections of poems—most recently, *Taken Somehow by Surprise* (2011)—and two book-length poems. He directs the creative writing program and coordinates the attendant Visiting Writer Series at Webster University, which he started in 1986. He was the poet laureate of Missouri from 2010 to 2012.

Brendan Constantine has served as a teacher of poetry in local schools and colleges since 1995. He is the author of five collections of poetry, including his most recent, *Bouncy Bounce* (2018). A popular performer, Constantine has presented his work to audiences throughout the U.S. and Europe, also appearing on NPR's *All Things Considered*, numerous podcasts, and YouTube.

C. S. E. Cooney is an audiobook narrator, the singer/songwriter Brimstone Rhine, and author of the World Fantasy Award–winning *Bone Swans: Stories*. Winner of the Rhysling Award for her poem "The Sea King's Second Bride," she is also the author of the novella *Desdemona and the Deep*, the poetry collection *How to Flirt in Faerieland and Other Wild Rhymes*, and other short fiction.

Kyle Dargan is the author of *Anagnorisis* (2018) in addition to four previous collections of poetry. He has received the Cave Canem Poetry Prize, the Hurston/Wright Legacy Award, and grants from the D.C. Commission on the Arts and

Humanities. He is an associate professor of literature and assistant director of creative writing at American University, as well as the founder and editor of *POST NO ILLS* magazine.

Jesse De Angelis lives in Boston. His poems have appeared in the *Kenyon Review* and *Best New Poets 2016*, among others.

Alison Hawthorne Deming is the author most recently of the poetry collection *Stairway to Heaven* (2016) and *Death Valley: Painted Light* (2016), a collaboration with photographer Stephen Strom. The recipient of a Guggenheim Fellowship, she is a Regents' Professor and Agnese Nelms Haury Chair of Environment and Social Justice at the University of Arizona. She lives in Tucson, Arizona, and Grand Manan, New Brunswick, Canada.

Bryan D. Dietrich is an American poet interested in science, science fiction, and pop culture, with several books and awards to his credit, including the collection *Krypton Nights* (2002) and the *Isotope* Editors' Prize. He lives in Kansas and teaches at Newman College.

Ronald Duncan (1914–82) was a British librettist, screenwriter, pacifist, poet, and playwright who wrote several books, including a long work about science called *Man* (1970–74).

Loren Eiseley (1907–77) was an anthropologist and one of the most important nature writers of the twentieth century, publishing such brooding, seminal works as *The Night Country* (1971), *The Immense Journey* (1957), and his balanced, lyrical critique of the space program, *The Invisible Pyramid* (1971). He also published three poetry collections.

Elaine V. Emans lived in Minneapolis. She was the author of *About Spiders: Introducing Arachne* (1940), *Earth's Child* (1950), and *Love Letter to the Blue Planet* (1992).

The first winner of the Emily Dickinson Award from the Poetry Foundation, **Landis Everson** (1926–2007) was part of the Berkeley Renaissance. He stopped writing for more than four decades before returning to poetry in 2003. His collected poems appeared in 2006, the year before he died.

The British poet **John Fairfax** (1930–2009) edited an anthology of space poetry called *Frontier of Going* (1969). He edited poetry at Phoenix Press and is rumored to have a poem in a time capsule on the Moon.

Keith Flynn is a musician and poet, having recorded three albums with The Crystal Zoo and having published seven books. He has won the Sandburg Prize and is managing editor of *The Asheville Poetry Review*.

Forrest Gander has authored books of poetry, novels, essays, and translations, including *Be With*, which won the 2019 Pulitzer Prize for Poetry. The recipient of grants from the Library of Congress and the Guggenheim, Howard, Whiting, and United States Artists Foundations, he taught for many years as the A. K. Seaver Professor of Literary Arts and Comparative Literature at Brown University.

Allen Ginsberg (1926–97) was America's pre-eminent Beat poet, best known for his controversial poem "Howl," which both distilled and shouted experiences and critiques of American culture and politics. Ginsberg's poetry energetically moves across subjects and almost performs itself on the page. Combining the intensely personal with the politics of the day and Eastern mysticism, Ginsberg's work remains some of the most notable in the twentieth century.

Nikki Giovanni is a major American writer who has authored twenty-eight books. She has been awarded seven NAACP Image Awards, and her album *The Nikki Giovanni Poetry Collection* was nominated for a Grammy. This *New York Times* best-selling author has for decades given voice to the experiences of African Americans, women in particular, and is an advocate of space exploration. She is a University Distinguished Professor of English at Virginia Tech.

Laurence Goldstein is a poet, critic, and former long-time editor of *Michigan Quarterly Review*, which published a special issue in 1979 titled "The Moon Landing and its Aftermath." He is the author of several books of poetry, including *A Room in California* (2005) from which the poem included in this anthology is taken.

Peter Milne Greiner is the author of *Lost City Hydrothermal Field* (2017), his debut collection of speculative poetry and prose. He guest-edited a critical science fiction issue of *Big Echo*, and he works with The Operating System, a New York publisher of avant-garde work.

Corrinne Clegg Hales is the author of five poetry collections, most recently *To Make it Right* (2011). Her work has been recognized with fellowships from the National Endowment for the Arts, the Devil's Millhopper Chapbook Prize, and the River Styx International Poetry Prize. Hales coordinates the Philip Levine Prize for Poetry annual book contest at California State University, Fresno.

Robert Hayden (1913–80) was a twentieth-century American poet and writer known for such poems as "Middle Passage" and "Those Winter Sundays." He was the first African American poet to hold the position of consultant in poetry at the Library of Congress, now the poet laureate title. He wrote many books of poetry, work that was much grounded in the Black experience, though he chafed against being identified in any way other than as simply a writer.

Mohja Kahf was born in Damascus, Syria, in 1967 to parents who immigrated to the United States in 1971. She is the author of two collections of poetry, *Hagar Poems* (2016) and *E-mails from Scheherazad* (2003), and a novel, *The Girl in the Tangerine Scarf* (2006). She is a professor of English at the University of Arkansas.

Donna Kane is the author of the poetry chapbook *Pioneer 10, I Hear You* (2016). She has also published two collections of poetry and a collection of nonfiction, *Summer of the Horse* (2018). She lives in northern British Columbia, where she works as executive director of the Peace Liard Regional Arts Council.

Douglas Kearney has published six books, most recently, *Buck Studies* (2016). He has received a Whiting Award, as well as residencies and fellowships from Cave Canem, the Robert Rauschenberg Foundation, and others. Raised in Altadena, California, he lives with his family near Minneapolis. He teaches creative writing at the University of Minnesota Twin Cities.

X. J. Kennedy translates, edits, and writes for children and adults. His poetry has been collected in several volumes, including *In a Prominent Bar in Secaucus: New and Selected Poems, 1955–2007*. According to the Poetry Foundation, "The Kennedy universe is engaging, humorous, and full of chaos." Kennedy is also the author of textbooks for writing and literature students.

Maxine Kumin (1925–2014) wrote nonfiction, novels, children's literature, and poetry, including eighteen volumes in the latter genre. A poetry consultant to the

Library of Congress, Kumin also won a Pulitzer Prize. Striving to balance writing with then-standard social expectations for women to be wives and mothers, Kumin would become a well-known writer, teacher, and champion of other female poets.

Twice poetry consultant to the Library of Congress and once poet laureate, **Stanley Kunitz** (1905–2006) published nearly two dozen works of poetry, criticism, and translation during a long and accomplished life. His vigorous opposition to censorship helped lead to the American Library Association's "Library Bill of Rights."

Gwyneth Lewis served as Wales's national poet from 2005 to 2006, the first to be given the Welsh laureateship. She has published eight collections of poetry in both English and Welsh. Lewis is also a librettist, dramatist, and nonfiction writer. She is a fellow of the Royal Society of Literature and The Welsh Academy.

Archibald MacLeish (1892–1982) was a prolific modernist writer and public servant—working for a time as assistant secretary of state for cultural affairs—known for an intellectually inclined approach to both individual and social experiences. In addition to his front-page poem on the first moon landing, the *New York Times* also published his essay on the Apollo 8 mission.

Adrian Matejka is the author of four collections of poetry, including his most recent, *Map to the Stars* (2017). His work has been recognized with fellowships from the Guggenheim and Lannan Foundations, and he has also been a finalist for the Pulitzer Prize for Poetry. He teaches at Indiana University in Bloomington and is poet laureate of Indiana.

Mark A. McCutcheon is from Toronto. He lives in Edmonton and teaches English literature at Athabasca University. McCutcheon's poems and short stories are published or forthcoming in literary magazines like *On Spec*, *Event*, *UnLost*, *Existere*, and *subTerrain*. His literary criticism appears in *The Explicator*, *Continuum*, *Extrapolation*, and other scholarly journals.

Campbell McGrath is the author of ten books, including his most recent *XX: Poems for the Twentieth Century* (2016). He has received numerous prestigious awards for his poetry, including a MacArthur Foundation "genius grant" and a Guggenheim Fellowship. He teaches in the MFA program at Florida International University and lives with his family in Miami Beach.

Patrick McGuinness is a professor of French and comparative literature at the University of Oxford, St. Anne's College. He is a poet, critic, and novelist. He published *The Canals of Mars*, his first poetry volume, in 2004. His novel *The Last Hundred Days* was nominated for the Man Booker Prize in 2011.

Lo Kwa Mei-en is the author of two poetry collections, *The Bees Make Money in the Lion* (2016) and *Yearling* (2015), winner of the Kundiman Poetry Prize, as well as two chapbooks. A poet from Singapore and Ohio, she lives and works in Cincinnati.

N. Scott Momaday is Kiowa, and his 1969 Pulitzer Prize–winning novel *The Way to Rainy Mountain* was the beginning of a long and distinguished career and an origin point of what has been called the Native American Renaissance. Winner of a National Medal of Arts, Momaday has published nearly twenty books to much acclaim.

Anthony Michael Morena is a writer from New York who lives in Tel Aviv. He is the author of *The Voyager Record: A Transmission* (2016) and assistant fiction editor for *Gigantic Sequins*. His writing has appeared in *The Establishment*, *Ninth Letter*, and others, including the *Ilanot Review*, where he has also been a guest editor and interviewer.

Hailed as one of Scotland's most important twentieth-century poets, **Edwin Morgan** (1920–2010) published an enormous number of books, including *Collected Poems* (1990). Influenced by the Beats, Morgan was much lauded and awarded, including winning a T. S. Eliot Prize for Poetry.

Tomás Q. Morín is the author of *Patient Zero* (2017) and *A Larger Country* (2012). He is co-editor with Mari L'Esperance of the anthology *Coming Close: 40 Essays on Philip Levine* (2013) and translator of *The Heights of Macchu Picchu* by Pablo Neruda. He teaches at Drew University and in the low-residency MFA program of Vermont College of Fine Arts.

Lisel Mueller (1924–2020) was born in Hamburg, Germany. Her books of poetry include *Alive Together: New and Selected Poems* (1996), which won the Pulitzer Prize; *The Need to Hold Still* (1980), which received the National Book Award; and *The Private Life*, which was the 1975 Lamont Poetry Selection.

Story Musgrave is a retired astronaut perhaps best known for his role in repairing the Hubble Space Telescope. A physician by training, Musgrave flew on all five space shuttle orbiters and has six academic degrees, including a master's degree in literature.

Howard Nemerov (1920–91) was a well-known poet of the twentieth century, the author of many books, and a long-time professor at Washington University in St. Louis. Known for his skill in formalist work, Nemerov won a Pulitzer Prize, a National Book Award, and the Bollingen Prize for Poetry. He also served twice as poetry consultant to the Library of Congress.

Pablo Neruda (1904–73) was one of the world's most important poets in the twentieth century. Widely translated from his native Chilean, Neruda won the Nobel Prize in Literature and was a diplomat and political activist. Controversial as a Communist, Neruda has been considered the national poet of Chile.

Hannah Faith Notess is the author of *The Multitude* (2015) as well as the poetry chapbook *Ghost House* (2013). She is the editor of *Jesus Girls: True Tales of Growing Up Female and Evangelical* (2009). She has served as the managing editor of Seattle Pacific University's *Response* magazine and currently works as a web developer.

Carolyn Oliver is a writer, poet, and editor. Her writing has appeared or is forthcoming in *Field*, *Indiana Review*, the *Greensboro Review*, *Tin House Online*, and others. A former teacher, she also works with a wide range of clients on writing and editing projects. Oliver lives in Massachusetts with her family.

Matthew Olzmann is the author of two collections of poems, *Mezzanines* (2013), which was selected for the Kundiman Poetry Prize, and *Contradictions in the Design* (2016). He's received fellowships from Kundiman, Kresge Arts in Detroit, and the Bread Loaf Writers' Conference. He teaches at Dartmouth College and in the MFA Program for Writers at Warren Wilson College.

Frank Paino's first two volumes of poetry are *The Rapture of Matter* (1991) and *Out of Eden* (1997). He has received several awards for his work, including a 2016 Individual Excellence Award from the Ohio Arts Council, a Pushcart Prize, and the Cleveland Arts Prize in Literature. Orison Books will publish Paino's third book, *Obscura*, in 2020.

Srikanth Reddy is the author of two collections of poetry, including *Voyager* (2011), as well as a book of literary criticism, *Changing Subjects: Digressions in Modern American Poetry* (2012). The National Endowment for the Arts and the Creative Capital Foundation have awarded him grants and fellowships, and in fall 2015 he served as a lecturer for the Bagley Wright Lecture Series on Poetry. He is currently an associate professor of English at the University of Chicago.

Adrienne Rich (1929–2012) published more than two dozen volumes of poetry and more than a half dozen volumes of prose throughout her lifetime. A leading poet, public intellectual, and feminist of her generation, her work was recognized with two National Book Awards, a MacArthur Fellowship, and a Medal for Distinguished Contribution to American Letters by the National Book Foundation.

Kim Stanley Robinson is a popular and influential figure in science fiction, lauded for his ability to craft narratives with nuanced characters, compelling ideas, accurate science, and political and philosophical implications. Among his many novels, some of the most crucial are those of the Mars Trilogy (1992–96), *2312* (2012), and *Aurora* (2015). He has been named a *Time* magazine "Hero of the Environment."

Elizabeth Lindsey Rogers is the author of *Chord Box* (2013), finalist for a Lambda Literary Award, and *The Tilt Torn Away from the Seasons* (2020). Rogers was the Murphy Visiting Fellow in English at Hendrix College from 2016 to 2019. She is a contributing editor at the *Kenyon Review* and a volunteer for the Veterans Writing Project.

Raymond Roseliep (1917–83) was a writer of haiku and a Catholic priest. In 1981, his sequence, "The Morning Glory," was placed on more than two thousand New York City buses. He published nineteen collections.

Mary Jo Salter is a poet, editor, essayist, playwright, and lyricist, whose work is associated with the New Formalist revival among contemporary American poets. She is co-editor of the influential *Norton Anthology of Poetry* and teaches at Johns Hopkins University. Salter has published seven books of poetry, among other works.

Anne Sexton (1928–74) was a pioneering poet of the 1960s Confessional movement, blending bracing feminist expressions of personal experience with daring poetic skill. Winner of the 1967 Pulitzer Prize for Poetry for her collection *Live or*

Die, Sexton is notable as a poet of profound and complicated interiority. She wrote many books before her suicide at age forty-six.

Enid Shomer is the author of four books of poetry and three of fiction, most recently the novel *The Twelve Rooms of the Nile* (2012). Her work has been collected in more than fifty anthologies and textbooks, and she is the editor of the poetry anthology *All We Know of Pleasure: Poetic Erotica by Women* (2018).

Four-time U.S. national slam poetry winner **Patricia Smith** is not only a poet but a former journalist, teacher, and playwright. She is the winner of many awards, including a Guggenheim Fellowship, and has published seven collections of poetry. She is a professor at the College of Staten Island, and she also teaches with the Vermont College of Fine Arts and Sierra Nevada College.

The 22nd U.S. Poet Laureate **Tracy K. Smith** is also the winner of the Pulitzer Prize for Poetry for *Life on Mars* (2011). She is the author of three additional poetry collections and a memoir, *Ordinary Light* (2015). Smith is director of Princeton's Program in Creative Writing and the chair of the university's Lewis Center for the Arts.

'Annah Sobelman (1954–2017) published two collections of poetry, *The Tulip Sacrament* (1995) and *In the Bee Latitudes* (2012). Born and raised in Los Angeles, she lived for many years in Florence, Italy, and Taos, New Mexico. She founded and served as editor for the *Taos Review*.

Mary Ellen Solt (1920–2007) was an avant-garde visual or "concrete" poet during her career, using words to form mimetic shapes on the page. Author of several books and a scholar of modernist poetry, she directed the Polish Studies Center at Indiana University.

Naru Dames Sundar writes speculative fiction of all kinds. He has previously been a DJ, a composer, and a potter. When he isn't devouring books or writing, he enjoys music, art, and the redwoods of northern California, where he lives.

May Swenson (1913–89) was a prolific mid-twentieth-century poet who wrote enduring work that is gaining additional attention for its inventiveness and compassionate eye for detail. Born and buried in Logan, Utah, but a long-time resident of Long Island, Swenson wrote from precision into metaphysics, prompting poet Richard Howard to write that she shows us "the larger, warmer energies of earth."

D. M. Thomas is a British writer whose novel *The White Hotel* (1981) brought him to the wider attention he still commands. He published poetry and prose in the experimental British science-fiction magazine *New Worlds* and has published more than two dozen novels and poetry collections, along with acclaimed translations from Russian literature.

Brian Turner is a poet and memoirist who served seven years in the U.S. Army. He is the author of two poetry collections, including *Here, Bullet*, which was a *New York Times* "Editor's Choice" selection. He is the editor of *The Kiss* (2018), an anthology. Turner has been awarded a United States Artists Fellowship, an NEA Fellowship, and a Lannan Foundation Fellowship, among others.

Frederick Turner is the author of three science-fiction epic poems, *Apocalypse* (2016), *Genesis* (1988), and *The New World* (1985), along with multiple other works that utilize formal poetic elements such as meter and narrative. Formerly the editor of the *Kenyon Review*, Turner is Founders Professor of Arts and Humanities at the University of Texas in Dallas.

One of America's foremost twentieth-century novelists, **John Updike** (1932–2009) also wrote poetry collected in eight books. His poems could be mistaken as light verse, but the work was often witty, musical, and precise. He is one of the few modern American novelists who wrote poetry with accomplishment and verve.

Peter Viereck (1916–2006) won the Pulitzer Prize for Poetry and wrote many books to both high praise and stinging criticism, a result of his verbal wit and formal mastery. A historian and political theorist, the *New York Times* describes Viereck as "a founder of the mid-20th-century American conservative movement who later denounced what he saw as its late-20th-century excesses."

William Wenthe, a poet and professor at Texas Tech University, is the author of four books of poetry, including his most recent, *God's Foolishness* (2016). A critic as well, he has won awards from the National Endowment for the Arts and the Texas Institute of Letters.

William Carlos Williams (1883–1963) is one of the most important poets to have written in English. A dominant and influential figure, Williams focused on precise imagery and playful experiments with lines and line breaks. Many students have been subjected to his famous poem "The Red Wheelbarrow," which is a poem perhaps best encountered when one is older. Of English and Puerto Rican descent, Williams was a practicing physician.

Raymond Wilson (1925–95) was a professor, editor, critic, and poet at the University of Reading, England.

Al Worden (1932–2020) was the command module pilot for Apollo 15, the first heavily scientific mission of the crewed lunar program. Upon his return he wrote a volume of verse called *Hello Earth: Greetings from Endeavor* (1974), one of the few poetic documentations by actual astronauts. Worden went on to write the compelling astronaut memoir *Falling to Earth* (2011).

POEM CREDITS